WITHIN MY SPOKES

A TAPESTRY OF PAIN, GROWTH & FREEDOM

JENNA UDENBERG

ISBN: 979-8-88759-811-6 - paperback

ISBN: 979-8-88759-812-3 - ebook

This memoir is dedicated to the lives that have made me who I am today:
my parents, siblings, family, adopted family and dear friends.

To you the reader:
I hope you find shared experiences, new adventures, and curious perspectives so we can grow together on this journey of sharing parts of my life. Happy reading!

Table of Contents

Introduction

Since childhood, I have been told to write a book due to enduring the good, bad, and painful memories of growing up with a medical condition. People suggested the book should contain all the funny stories that one can not make up as seen from the perspective of 4' 2". Others told me to write my book about the deep faith that drives my perseverance in living life to the fullest, while making an impact for the generations behind me.

Writing all of this has been a journey. The more one knows themself the more they know the world around them. The more comfortable I became in my own body and wheels, the more comfortable I became asking questions of others about their bodies and wheels or lack of wheels. Also putting my memories and experiences to the written word has brought up some past and childhood traumas that are shared here, while some are still tucked away and not for sharing... yet. Reliving some of these situations has been an activity in self reflection, and in awe of my Lord who has provided MUCH healing throughout my journey thus far. I share details and stories I didn't think were possible or needed, only to be reassured that those details are the whole crux of my story.

Chapter 1
The Unraveling

"Hard things are put in our way, not to stop us, but to call out our courage and strength."- Unknown

My story begins in the bathtub. It was midwinter of 1987 and I was seven years old, almost eight. The baby of the family with three siblings that were much older... twelve, fifteen and sixteen years older to be exact. My life was a happy one living in my family's love and warmth sprinkled with regular teasing and good fun. I reveled in bugging my much older siblings and I loved school. We lived on the outskirts of city limits with a big yard and trees, where sightings of deer, bear, and even coyotes weren't rare. Our town had a few more bars than churches and nestled up to beautiful Lake Superior. On that cold winter morning in our big golden bathtub filled with toys and bubbles, playing in my own little world, my right knee, the size of a volleyball, floated to the top of the water. I stared. Then quickly pulled up my left knee to compare the two. The left was its usual tennis ball size. So I did what any little kid would do, I screamed for my mom!

The story, as I have been told countless times, but do not remember, is that we went ice skating the day before and I had a fall. So after my vivid morning bath my memory becomes a blur. I saw the doctor who helped deliver me and my dad did not like everything he had to say so I ended up seeing another doctor in town. He took one look at me and my bloodwork and said he thought I had a disease called Juvenile Rheumatoid Arthritis (JRA). These were some big words that meant I was sick with a disease that typically only old people get when their hands and legs don't want to work right anymore. But our town doctor didn't feel comfortable prescribing a course of treatment for me so we had to go to the big city, Duluth, to see a rheumatologist. From here I had to go down to the Mayo Clinic in Rochester, MN. Since Lyme Disease was new on the scene and many of the symptoms of JRA and Lyme's were similar, I had to go through a whole battery of tests.

Well to this little second grader who thought Duluth was the big city, my mind was completely blown in Rochester and at Mayo Clinic. I remember seeing many different doctors with very thick accents from other countries. I had a very hard time understanding the adult words, the medical terms and then keeping up with the fast-paced accented words, too. I remember many x-rays, bloodwork sessions, and the horrible barium scans. I have a texture issue so drinking anything that is thick or grainy drives my tongue bonkers, which then made the radiology tech very angry and terse with me because I made him fall behind schedule. Until my wonderful, protective father corrected this guy's thinking about putting his little girl first, not the radiologist's precious schedule. Seeing my dad speak low and quietly while being in this man's personal bubble made me feel very uncomfortable, so I quickly chugged the barium as to not be the reason for any further anger. Deep inside, my dad's actions made me feel safe and watched over.

I remember being confused a lot in all the different sessions and just being easily distracted by all the new environments and experiences. I am sure my blankie was probably nearby as words swirled around me in accents and terms I could not understand, yet. One doctor gave my parents some aspirin for me to take while we were out at lunch. Now this place was fancy! I remember looking at this weird man all dressed up for lunch in a tux or suit and there was carpeting on the floor!!! Next I remember my mom having to crush the pills with spoons before mixing them in my mashed potatoes. I tried to warn my parents saying I know I am going to puke these up if you make me eat them in my mashed potatoes. I got the typical mother look of "Child, do what I say because this is what's best for you." Well, I remember the carpeting cause my tongue defied my mother's look and won the battle.

After this memorable lunch we went back to see another doctor. This time it was different. Exam tables were replaced with expensive looking leather furniture and a big dark brown desk with matching oak shelves. This doctor also had no accent and was smiling, mostly. He confirmed what our small town doctor had told us weeks or months earlier. Our lives changed forever in those few moments but I was excited to get a lollipop from the nice man. I understood the doctor's words, but not the sadness that left the office with us.

Juvenile Rheumatoid Arthritis (JRA) is an auto-immune disease that tricks your immune system into thinking that the cartilage in your joints is an infection or foreign body that must be removed. As a child I would describe this as a messed up disease that caused my body to eat my joints instead of eating the cold or flu virus or bugs that typical children get. It causes lots of inflammation which then causes joint damage, lack of movement, lots of pain, and eventually destroys the joint and other soft tissue structures around it. As a child I would always use the example of checking out your grandparents' hands as arthritis is mostly considered an old person's disease. This example helped them know that I wasn't contagious because their grandparents aren't contagious.

Who knew the memory of the expensive looking office and the lollipop would be the moment that became the pivotal dividing line of how my whole life would be talked about and remembered.

Even in current conversations with my family, my elementary schooling is labeled with the time marker of a "good year" or a "bad year" as well as if it was before or after I was sick. This isn't right or wrong, it just is. We humans use labels as placeholders to mark times of significant change. My whole school history was characterized and memorized by my painful and disabling disease:

Kindergarten: lots of fun, painting, watching boys eat paste, wooden trucks and kitchens, story time. Before I was sick.

First grade: a cardboard house for friends to read *See Dick Run*, a Halloween story using lettuce for brains and cold cooked spaghetti in a paper bag for the stomach. Before I was sick.

Second grade: scratch and sniff stickers for jobs well done. My dad lifted me on the bus each morning when he was home because I couldn't walk stairs anymore. There was a bully on the bus who got removed because of his hurtful words to me. I missed more school than I was at school. When I got sick.

First day of school in rental wheelchair. 1988

Third grade: I had my first wheelchair that we rented. Also I had serial casts on my legs trying to keep my knees straight. During this time the casts gave me the stability to "walk." So I was the cool kid when I could evacuate my wheels and other friends got to try them out. My class-mates thought a wheelchair was cool until their arms started to hurt or until it took more time to accomplish a task that they could do easier as a non-wheelie. After I was sick.

Fourth grade: I was assigned a certain teacher in August but since they were not friendly to "kids like me" I had a new teacher assignment before school started. Sitting in my chair at the table in the front of the classroom when I was able to be at school. Bad year. After I was sick.

Childhood Trauma

> *Experts say that when one has trauma in childhood, parts of their psyche are stunted at the age of the trauma. I would say that this is true but it can be healed and worked through as I have experienced. Sometimes this needs the help of medical and mental health professionals, and sometimes it just needs prayer, patience, and safe places to work through these struggles. For me there wasn't anything one person did or any fault to my family or friends, it was just the way life is or was when you are a child with a severe medical illness. I am thankful to see the medical model changing in these regards. There are now patient advocates and child life experts in many hospitals. The medical world also now acknowledges that a medical change in a child does not just affect the child but the whole family and community. There are growing numbers of support for these needs. And yet, in some of the pediatric illness support systems it seems as if the medical world*

is just treating the disease with medications. They think kids with JRA are fine and don't see themselves as different because the meds make them "better." But in reality, that isn't the whole patient andisn't a healthy approach to helping the family unit cope and thrive with the unexpected lifestyle changes impacting their lives.

Even if medications stop the pain and joint destruction, it doesn't take away the feeling of being different, the side effects of harsh meds, or the atypical schedule of many more doctor appointments, procedures, and therapies compared to healthy peers. The times of hospitalizations and surgeries that made me feel isolated and estranged from your family can many times make you feel abandoned and unwanted. Your life as a young person is filled with lots of random strangers that you meet who poke, prod and ask embarrassing questions of you. You quickly learn how to navigate the adult world as you are constantly in it but you struggle in navigating life with your peers because each of you can not understand the world the other lives in. You learn to make quick relationships with these adults that flash through your life because if they see you as a fellow human they will treat you better and be more careful with the body parts that cause you pain. You also learn how to self advocate very quickly because there are some people that are not in the right careers for them and they hurt you through no fault of your own.

Fifth grade: In order to learn about the respiratory system in science class, our teacher had us bring in deer lungs during the deer hunting season. My family is full of avid hunters and outdoorsmen so we had many extra deer lungs to explore that year. That year also included the "talk." My desk was a table in the back of the room.

My first time in medical rehab in Duluth, my social studies teacher came to visit me in the hospital. I gave him a super sour candy by tricking him and hoping he wouldn't "erupt" as this is how he kept his classroom management in check, by not erupting. We had a big laugh at this.

During this stay I was getting my new medication levels figured out and helping my body through a JRA flare up, which is when my body gets very hot, the affected joint(s) get very swollen, achy, and lose function or strength. All of this pain can cause great exhaustion and brain fog too, which can make me overemotional. When all the medical junk was done each day I played games with kids my own age, and other times I would play games with folks like grandparents to me. Andrea, a Rehab Recreation Specialist, made my first experience with medical rehab go very well. Many days I and my two young friends couldn't wait for the painful doldrums of the daytime therapies to be over so we could play balloon basketball on a gurney in the hall with Andrea. This also was near Christmas time so I have pictures by the Christmas tree with my new friend Darla who became my penpal for a few years after rehab. She was the first adult I had met that also used a wheelchair and had JRA. It felt weird meeting an "old" person with a kid's disease, but it was also comforting to meet an "old" person still alive with JRA because it showed me there was life and a quality to life no matter what this disease did to me. I was lucky to not spend the holiday in rehab but my two young friends weren't so lucky. I think of Andrea, Darla, and these two friends often and wonder where life has found them. Maybe some-day our paths will cross again, and even if they don't, their footprints and wheel marks are on my heart and journey.

This year was not super bad but not a great one either.

Sixth grade: Our chairs with wheels race between me and my homeroom teacher in the hallway. He was in his office chair going back-wards and I was in my wheelchair. I would have lost big time BUT a classmate jumped out and held the teacher's chair which kept him from winning.

During this time my right elbow was fusing, which is when the disease damages the joint and cartilage so bad that motion and function stop. This was VERY painful and it could not bend very easily. I had to learn how to brush my hair and teeth using my left hand in a mirror! I started beginning band by playing my oldest sister's cornet, a trumpet-like instrument. But due to the right elbow pain and limited function, I flipped my hands to play my cornet as a leftie even though my trumpet playing band teacher told me there were no left handed trumpet players. In addition to band we had recorder class. In order to fully play the plastic recorder one has to put their left hand on top and their thumb and 3 fingers cover the small holes. Their right hand also covers 3-4 small holes depending on the notes they are playing. The right hand has the most weight to hold up while your elbow is bent so your hand is about 6 inches away from your mouth.

Sixth grade was a hard year for me and I needed extra physical therapy (PT) to help manage my flare up. This was a whole body flare with constant hot flashes as every joint was angry with swelling and pain. So I always missed recorder class as that is when the PT could see me. She treated me in the sick bay of the nurse's office, me with an autoimmune disease in a flare up. (Hopefully these things are not happening in our current schools to protect the PT patient as well as the sick students, but I digress.) So when report cards came out I received an F for recorder class. My usually easy going parents and I, the typical A student, were not happy.

The only day I ever got called down to the principal's office was the day my parents came in to complain to get my grade removed or reversed, because how can a student who is never in class because of scheduling be punished for things outside of their control? I remember that being a very uncomfortable time as the principal called the teacher, whom I had only met a few times, down to his office with my parents in the room, too. Needless to say, my grade was changed. A good year considering.

Chapter 2

The Quirky Creative

"When we talk about education, it's very important that when we say 'all,' we mean 'all.'"
- Judith Heumann

In seventh grade we became the first class to get moved to the big high school! Typically high school is for students in 9th to12th grade so moving seventh graders who are only 12 years old to be with 18 year-olds is scary. There were building reconfigurations due to population changes and budget cuts so I found myself in the big, not very accessible high school. Lots of wheeling and using a freight elevator with an old creaky pull gate that was wreaking of oil and mechanical smells. It had no ceiling so you could watch all of the cables and floors above you. Some teachers showed acceptance and others had no time for me.

As a younger person using a wheelchair in a small rural town in the days before the internet, there was little chance to be immersed in disability culture. I remember a young man with cerebral palsy who used a power chair and a young girl who used crutches. They were a few years younger than me and were mainstreamed for most of their classes. We usually only saw each other on the accessible bus and in passing from the special ed room where our helpers, paraprofessionals (paras), worked. There were a few other young men who used wheelchairs too, but they were nonverbal and isolated to the special ed room so I also only saw them briefly on the bus and when I was in the room to grab a para. Sometimes I saw them when I was putting my book bag or supplies on a chair inside the door for lunch and band times, so I could have my hands free for lunch trays and trumpet cases. These young friends always intrigued me but also made me feel sad because of the opportunities they seemed to be missing out on when it came to school and friends.

In my medical world there were big changes too.I got a new physical therapist. Lisa was a fresh out of PT school, highly energized, positive person while I was an angry, hurting middle school kid facing an elbow that was fusing and knees and ankles that never stopped hurting. She introduced me to pool therapy which is a workout while having fun in a pool that is a cross between a nice warm bath and a hot tub with jets! It gave me freedoms of movement I could never have on land. It also gave me a new and unique friend, Jaime.

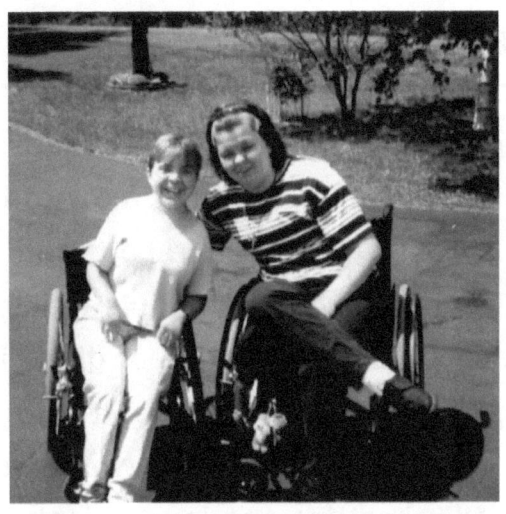

Jaime and I at my graduation party , 1998.

Jaime is a fellow wheelie due to JRA. A "wheelie," is a disability culture term for a fellow person who uses a wheelchair. It is a label I am comfortable with for myself with my friends who are also in disability culture. While our medical stories differ a little, much of our stories are very similar. Jaime was diagnosed at age two which was much younger than me, but our family structures and functions have great similarities.

Jaime was the adventurous one going to camp, playing wheelchair basketball, dating, being in plays, enjoying life in community to the fullest. I was a quiet, tentative, cautious, ok...scaredy cat.

Jaime pushed me out of my comfort zones in engaging with people and entering disability culture through joining a local junior wheelchair basketball team. Now this was my true introduction to disability culture. Don't get me wrong, I had been in and out of physical rehabs and medical settings for rehabilitation multiple times a week and saw many different forms of disability from birth to grave. But the medical setting of disability has its own flare and norms, where being out of the medical setting and in an adaptive sports setting is a whole new world.

As a 13 year-old kid who was just trying to figure out my weird body with all the new hormones, medications, and my disease, going into a new activity with new people was a whole new level of Jumanji scary for me. Everyone seemed to know each other because they were all from the "big city" of Duluth and I was the unknown country bumpkin from the little town north of them. I would try not to stare, but I would also try to figure out my new teammates' diagnosis or their needs.

I knew the game of basketball very well, or so I thought, as my oldest sister had played ball and was coaching our high school teams. I loved the NBA and watched the Chicago Bulls whenever I could. I really admired Scottie Pippen #33 even though everyone else went with Micheal Jordan #23. So I chose #33 to be my jersey number. Once I got to practices, I realized that wheelchair basketball was no joke and this was going to physically kick my butt.

We used a women's size basketball. The basketball hoops were usually at regular height but sometimes they were lowered if we were working on different skills or needs. I was a pretty portly kid since I had been in a chair for about five years at this point and I had been on prednisone on and off for those years. Prednisone is an amazing medication but it has the horrible side effect of creating the seefood diet: when you see it, you eat it. Plus being in tremendous amounts of pain and swelling made me not want to move, let alone move rapidly to get a cardio workout. I was still getting used to my right arm being fused almost straight so wheeling down the court became my goal as to not be the last player in the zingers warm-ups.

We did the typical basketball line-to-line zingers to warm up. Learning how to stop on a dime and turn on a dime was crucial. We could get fouls if our chairs were perceived to ram into the opposing players. So developing intricate wheelwork, like footwork, was a high goal. I also became very knowledgeable and aware of my different wheelchair parts. I had both feet plates on for basketball, but for me to move fast down the court I would have my left foot up on the plate and my right foot down to help propel and steer. I twisted my knee and ankle in such a way that the outer part of my right foot pressed on the nut of my right caster which would make me glide or turn without the use of my hands. Having my left leg up created a flat surface for the ball to rest on when I had possession. I tried everything to be able to shoot the ball, but my strength and lack of height were my biggest limitations. Trying to do a "jump shot" from about three to four feet high with little vertical movement is WAY harder than the Paralympians make it look. I am sure the beginning of my hand and wrist issues were also a part of this adaptive process. I was always in awe of my teammates without arm limitations that just spun the ball and lobbed it in as if they were Jordan or O'Neal. My brain could just not figure out how to make my body do what their's did. I kept trying to do granny shots or other unorthodox ways of getting that ball to the fateful rim as I always got net, just never the net after the rim...haha. Well one day I tried to modify a move I saw in a Bulls game by throwing the ball from my fused right arm and voila...I hit the rim!!! This hook shot became my only real basketball move. I tried to score many times but I can not remember if I ever made a shot when it counted in a game. Trying to learn the angle of my hook shot, which was very static due to no elbow movement, was challenging. Everyone would cheer to shoot the ball, but many times I was not where I could lower the ball on the side without someone stealing it or I wasn't at the right angle for success. But this new ability sticks with me even today as I started calling my right arm my hook, which was short for hook shot. However, everytime I call it my hook around new people or strangers I have to tell them this story or they think I am like Captain Hook or have an artificial arm. I have had many dear friends when first getting to know me who do not feel comfortable with calling my right arm my hook. But after lots of discussion they begin to see that this name for my body part is one of acceptance and uniqueness not of hurt or shame.

These weekly practices were a strain on my schedule and on my mom as this was an added trip to the "big city" on top of the three days a week for my PT and doctor appointments. We spent LOTS of time on the road and basketball season is during our hardest and longest season here on the Shore- the never ending winter. Slowly I became more comfortable and didn't have to use Jaime as my shield and entry into conversations with others.

Traveling to our only tournament holds the most memories of all my wheelchair basketball days. This was my first trip away from home with no family adults to help me. Jaime had to convince my parents that she would take care of me and watch out for me. We were going to Camp Courage in the Twin Cities where Jaime had been going to summer camps since she was young. This was SCARY for me. Thrilling but also terrifying. We loaded the bus which was no small feat! Most of our players were semi-ambulatory, meaning they could walk a little or a lot but had an everyday wheelchair as well as a special sports chair for basketball. We had gear and parts everywhere, let alone all of our own bags and personal care equipment too. I remember traveling at night with music blaring and young people screaming and singing at the top of their lungs. Some of our teammates traveled down with family, but most of us were having loud bonding times on this very bumpy and uncomfortable school bus. I got to sit in a bus seat, as being strapped in my chair for the three to four hours to get to the cities would have been even worse than what I had endured in that cold, hard, unforgiving bus seat.

I have spotty memories of camp and the experience, but here are my highlights. I remember being in bunk beds. I had the bottom bunk of course. Camp was cold. I remember being intrigued as my neighbor was an amputee due to pediatric cancer so seeing her prosthetic leg standing by her bed at night time was a new one for me. My brain was overwhelmed seeing people of all heights, abilities, hair colors, and chair types. I vividly remember during the middle of a game seeing a very tall young man strapped into his basketball chair get rammed on the court. His chair flipped so he was face down on the floor with his butt and wheels up in the air. His green hair flapping in the wind as he got floor burns across his whole face from the aggressive foul. From that moment on I vowed to NEVER be strapped into my chair because for me the pain and injury of being stuck like that was far greater than flying out.

We celebrated the end of the tournament with a dance. I am a very shy and unsure person in new environments, but once I feel safe and a sense of belonging I don't stop talking. Seeing what felt like hundreds of chair users chair dancing in a variety of ways was a whole new experience. Many guys spinning until they were up on only one or two wheels. Popping wheelies on your back two tires, were old school tricks. And then seeing wheelies with non-wheelies sitting on their laps for slow dances was also a whole new world to me. I didn't have these words at the time but looking back I see this as my first realization that I really lived between two cultures and the dominant, non-disabled, medically-based world was far more impacting to me than this youth disability culture that felt foreign and yet intriguing to me.

During this tournament I also realized that all of the personality types that the non disabled world has, disability culture also has. AKA we can be jerks and worse, too. By and large our team and our coaches just wanted to go and have a good time. We would do our best and encourage each other to do so. However one of our teammates was focused more on winning and less on encouraging his fellow teammates. As such, I was usually the one in his crosshairs as I did not understand all of the plays and screens. Since I was not a scorer, my strength was as a picker. I would ram my feet plate or other wheelchair parts into the nooks and crannies of other people's chairs so our scoring players could get through the mess of metal to get to the hoop.

My teammates had diverse backgrounds, family dynamics, and levels of disability. Some were immersed in disability culture while others, like myself, were first timers. A few teammates only tolerated us so they could play ball. It was also interesting to me and a great learning experience to be coached by the older adult team players. I had never been around middle-aged people in chairs. I went from pediatric doctors offices and PT times to visiting elderly family members in the nursing home. There were no interactions with people in chairs just out in community living life.

Until now I had not met another person with JRA, besides Jaime. There was a quiet young man named Davis who shared our diagnosis. Davis had arm splints and, like me, had the prednisone baby face. We both looked much younger than we were. He always tried his best, but wheeling his chair took a lot of work for him. I had always wished that basketball season wasn't in the winter as JRA can be full of flare ups and lots of swelling and pain in our cold, snow filled months here in northern Minnesota. Davis and I only had a handful of conversations, but I always felt like we just understood each other even if very few words were used. Just a year or so after our trip to Camp Courage Davis lost his battle with JRA. His obituary mentioned complications with JRA. After losing him I did some research, Google didn't exist back then, and I found out that there can be a condition caused by JRA that impacts the lungs and can cause death. I knew that this disease betrayed me everyday but I had no idea it could also kill me. Now I understood why my rheumatologist always asked about my trumpet playing, not just because he too was a musician—a jazz piano player— but because he was checking on my lung capacity and function. Sneaky Dr.

Eighth grade: We called our new middle school band director Fitz, for short. Fitz was a short statured spit fire with a love of music education and all things middle school. She was a breath of fresh air to our teaching staff and put the beginning and middle school bands on the map for our small town. She truly saw me as a person with talent.

By this time my right elbow had been fully fused and I had become quite the cornet/trumpet player. In seventh grade, I was playing split lead, sharing the lead trumpet player role with an eighth grade boy in our middle school band. This surpassed my previous band director's expectations since he told me just a year before that there are no left handed cornet players. But once Fitz came and saw me playing I learned the bad news. I wasn't really reading the music rhythmically, I was succeeding by just playing what I heard. I knew all my note names and fingerings, but the rhythmic world alluded me. I remember the year before my split lead partner said he didn't read the music, notes or rhythms, he just knew the fingerings for each thing on the page and memorized the rhythms once the teacher played them for us. Being honest, I thought I was so much better because I knew the note names, fingerings, AND rhythms—or so I thought. Humble pie. To this day I am still not the best with rhythms but I can admit it and use the teachings I received all the way back in eighth grade and beyond to help address those gaps in my music playing.

Fitz and Cherne, our high school band director, worked together to start junior high jazz bands. They were a blast even though my rhythm issues caused anxiety for me and improvisation was scary in front of others. But Fitz and our high school band director saw things in me I didn't know I had. They worked together to groom me into a future lead trumpet player for the high school program. I have no idea why in our town we change or leave off the prefixes to some of our teachers but for me I think Fitz and Cherne truly became an inspiration for me, not just as a trumpet player and musician, but also in becoming a better human. They saw kids for who they were and didn't pull any punches or beat around the bush. Some did not like their approaches on certain things, but for me it was refreshing because I knew what was expected and there was consistency.

At the end of my eighth grade year, Cherne wanted me to get a real trumpet as I had been playing my older sister's hand-me-down cornet. I was proud to buy my trumpet all by myself and get a fun case that had shoulder straps. These straps made it easier for me to carry my instrument by myself unlike the usual hard molded instrument cases. I had a nice new shiny silver trumpet with mutes! This was my new prized possession.

Despite the huge amounts of accommodations and physical things they had to do for me, Fitz and Cherne were HUGE advocates for me to be in their band program. Our junior high and high school were housed in a building that was built in the 1950's, with no elevator to the band room located in the basement next to the wood boiler room. This was horribly unsafe and inhumane and would be (should be) unheard of today.

My sister helped me travel to a middle school youth rally where my youth director asked if he could introduce me to another girl with JRA. A shy redhead girl named Nic and her mom came over to meet me and my oldest sister. They were both nice and had great smiles. Nic was still walking, but I recognized the JRA signs of joint swelling and the way we hold our bodies, especially when we are in pain. We exchanged phone numbers and talked at times about what we were going through as well as about church and youth group things.

The Arthritis Foundation also paired me with a penpal in North Dakota who had JRA.

We communicated a few times, but writing letters can be very hard for someone with hurting and swollen hands. We lost touch, but I always wonder how she is and where she is. She is probably somewhere doing amazing work bettering this world. At least that is what I picture for her.

Reflection:

> Having penpals connected me with others like myself so I did not feel alone in my journey, and the writing helped work on my fine motor skills and hand strength. In today's technology and social media world, there are many more options as well as more accessible opportunities to share stories and build relationships.

Chapter 3

The Dark Night of the Soul

"Trust in the LORD with all your heart and lean not on your own understanding; in all your ways acknowledge Him, and He will make your paths straight…"

Proverbs 3:5-6 NIV

From seventh through ninth grade I had to use a stair trek chair to get downstairs twice a day to the band room. This scary contraption held my manual wheelchair to itself by two pinned levers attaching around my wheelchair's handlebars. I had a paraprofessional who was amazing and nice, but by her own words was "the oldest para with carpal tunnel."It was her job to connect me, pop a wheelie and then lift this whole machine, my wheelchair, and my personal weight up and over the top stair to guide it down the stairs. She had to make sure it didn't go too fast on the way down, and she had to help pull it up a bit on our trips back up after my band classes. Once I was down in the band room, then Fitz, Cherne, or some trusted high school students had to pop a wheelie and pull me up to the third riser where the trumpet section was seated. Being a freshman in the first trumpet section, sitting what felt like miles away from my fellow freshmen and in between the seniors, was intimidating to say the least. Since I was in the high school band and jazz band I had a separate lunch from most of my friends, so the senior girls in these ensembles took me under their wings.

I had just turned 15 years old and I was a hot mess in every sense of the word. I was in a huge arthritic flare. Everything hurt so much so that if someone even leaned against the side of my bed it hurt me. I was also a mess mentally and emotionally. This was back in the mid 1990's when mental health and depression were taboo topics. Each time my doctors asked about my mental health I would lie because I had to be strong for everyone else, or so I thought. I went what felt like months without going to school. I cried myself to sleep and eventually stopped taking my friends' calls. When I heard the phone ring after school I took all my might to flop myself towards my bedroom wall and fake sleep so mom would tell my friends I was sleeping. This worked pretty well. I did not realize what a bad situation I was in until one day my family decided that my black lab named Blackie (I was such an original five-year-old when I named my dog) needed to be put down. He had very bad arthritis and a big cancerous tumor that continued to grow back on his jaw. An extended family member came to put him down. I remember looking at my bedroom wall with tear-filled eyes at a black lab portrait wishing I too could be put out of my misery. Some of my family tried to "pull me out of my depression" with well intentioned words or actions, but many times they were just fire used to depress me and isolate me even more. I remember one day using wounding words as I fired back that my family could sell my newly purchased trumpet cause; I would never play again cause I would never leave that bedroom again. I felt bad after those words came flooding out with anger, rage, and hurt. But there was honesty in those words because school, band, and music seemed so far away and required enduring too much pain to get there. If someone leaning against my bed hurt so bad, how in the world could I ever do a bus ride to school...that would be pure torture and trauma.

The day my dog was put down was the day I cried out to Jesus. I had grown up in the local Lutheran church doing Tuesday School, Sunday School, church, and youth group. So I knew of God and I had served Him and His people, but I knew I needed more of Him. You see, I had a suicide plan to start stock piling my arthritis meds so I could try overdosing, and if that didn't work I was going to throw myself down our stairs to get to my father's gun cabinet. I was desperate for all the physical, mental, relational and spiritual pain to stop.

When I look back on these plans it is alarming, and yet my plan had such impossible steps. I couldn't get myself in my wheelchair by myself let alone throw myself down our split entry steps to then scoot to the larger basement steps. Then I would have to log roll on cement for like 50—100 feet to get to the gun cabinet. But the key would be over six feet in the air on top of the cabinet to then get a gun out after finding the separate ammunition. I only share these details to potentially help others see that even if suicide plans are not probable or logical to you right now, to the me in those moments, this plan was my only hope. I couldn't see all the problems or errors in my plan. My pain was so real and laying in that bed all I wanted was someone to climb in and truly experience it all with me. Isolation and chronic pain can be paralyzing, numbing and soul crushing. Even the well-meaning words and truths from my loved ones became fuel for my darkest thoughts because my thought processes were so dark, negative, and twisted.

So in my crying out to Jesus I remember saying, "God I love you and I have served you and I don't deserve you but I can not do this anymore. You have to do this cause I can not anymore. I don't want to end my life or go to hell or whatever happens to people like me. I NEED you and you are all I truly have." And then I experienced a peace I had never felt before, and truly resting and letting go.

After school that day I tried to do my usual fake sleeping but my mom caught me and told me I had to answer my friend's call. I was shocked when I answered the phone as it was my good friend Jenny who told me the devastating news that Fitz had a house fire. Thankfully she and her husband were safe but just devastated. My need to make sure she was ok was really the impetus for me to get out of my house and work to get back to school. I don't know how long it took me to accomplish this goal, but I made it. I remember this season and testimony yearly as it happened the day before the Oklahoma City bombing. I believe this also made me want to get back to my friends, school and my music, because life is SO short and our relationships are what truly matters in this life. Our whole world can be shaken at any moment from house fires, to medical issues, to acts of terrorism.

I wish I could say that I have never dealt with depression or isolation after this time but that would be untrue. I have never been to the depths like this season, but I have visited this pit from time to time as medical issues overwhelmed me or issues in relationships with my spiritually adopted or chosen family. But through each season I have come out stronger, more empathetic and compassionate for others and their struggles. I am also slowly learning to practice more grace for myself.

A few months after this suicide plan and finding a relationship with Jesus, I got a piece of mail from Lisa in Iowa. It was a birth announcement as she had become a mom to a beautiful little girl. Meeting this sweet girl one day and seeing Lisa again became reasons for me to fight through these dark and hard days. .

Even though Fitz and Cherne were technically only my teachers for one year in my musical career, they became like musical parents to me. When something musical in my life happened or was accomplished I wanted to share it with them. Cherne moved on to another local school after my freshman year and Fitz continued to play piano for me at contests each spring. Since my high school only had one wheelchair accessible school bus, which could not go out on field trips, Fitz was always nice and transported me to and from honor bands and contests in her personal stationwagon. This may have also led to secret trips through the Hardee's drive thru for fresh hot curly fries. Sometimes when you feel different because things are different for you, you have to embrace the extra perks. *These accommodations of having a teacher drive you in their personal vehicle would be unheard of today with liabilities and such, but these were the times of sharing life that built a friendship that has lasted for decades.*

There were great changes to the physical band world in my school starting my sophomore year. I had been injured from repetitive jolts from the stair trekker and I actually needed surgery. Because of my inability to use the stair trekker, we now had our high school jazz band on the auditorium stage with trumpets being on the stage level and the rest of the band being down in the orchestra pit area or on risers in the pit. Our high school band got moved to the first period of the day and our band met at our intermediate school three blocks away. The city revamped the curb cuts and sidewalks as needed for this three block stretch, so on good weather days my friends and I could walk with the other bandmates. On bad weather or hard days, the accessible school bus would return at the end of class to bring me to the high school for the rest of my school day.

It was hard interacting with some peers knowing they were not fans of the extra work or inconvenience of being in a different building, which allowed me to be in their band. I also learned a teacher or two were quite vocal to other teachers about having to do all this work "for just one kid." Fitz and our new high school director had my back and fought the fights that were needed without me knowing.

Chapter 4

The Wrong Leg and a Snake

"Contains Aftermarket Parts." - Unknown

Medically, my arthritis had gotten very bad. It now consumed my ankles, knees, one hip, and right elbow. My knees were the sources of my greatest pain in my early high school days. I had been seeing an orthopedic surgeon for adults for about a year. We were waiting for a pediatric orthopedic surgeon to move to Duluth from Canada but things kept getting waylaid in the adult bureaucracy world. So after months and months of waiting I got to meet this highly anticipated surgeon. After looking at my x-rays and doing a physical exam of my joints he looked at me and said, "Well, aren't you a pediatric orthopedic nightmare!" Now most people would be offended and probably would not come back, but there was something in this surgeon that I knew I could respect and trust. Plus I was like, "Yeah, duh. Try living in this self-betraying body! It is a nightmare, somedays!"

We scheduled my first surgery at age 16. The surgeons were concerned about growth plates in my knees as I wasn't fully grown yet, but I was close. My parents gave me the freedom to make these life and death medical decisions for myself months earlier, and for that I was grateful. After all, this was my body and my life journey that would be shaped and molded by every decision ahead. We were told very early on by my first physical therapist that once surgeries started on bodies like mine they would never stop. Once you start orthopedic or joint/muscle surgeries on young bodies, you have to keep doing surgeries to promote mobility as the young body grows and matures. Also, once you change the landscape of the function of one joint, that impacts the joints and tissues above and below the surgical joint. This advice weighed on me and was not forgotten.

I was scared to go into a surgery of this size. Up until this point I had only had a day surgery for bladder issues as a little girl. All I remember about that was getting a stuffed bear and popsicles afterwards for my sore throat. But ripping a knee open and cleaning it out. That would need more than a bear and popsicle to make me feel better.

I don't have many memories of this first surgery. I remember my mom came to the pre-op rooms to be my advocate with tears in her eyes. I do have post surgery memories, though. I woke up easy peasy. I was so impressed and was like if this is surgery then I am totally cool with it. But when I saw my parents' and surgeons' faces I knew something was not right.

When they put me on the surgery table they knocked me out and did some special scans before starting the procedure. The scans showed my knees were actually fully fused from the arthritis and I, or more likely the stair trekker used for getting to the band room, had created hairline fractures in my femur, the thigh bone. These hairline fractures gave me a few degrees of movement in my knees just weeks before the surgery. The surgeons were flabbergasted that my pain tolerance was SO high that I had no pain, and could actually move through a fracture to have some "joint" function.

I didn't have surgery that day, but just a little medicine induced nap for them to get good scans. They delivered the bad news that I needed total knee replacements, but since I was so young they didn't have all the needed parts for this new bionic knee. I would need both knees replaced during two different surgeries. I stayed in the hospital for a few days while we waited for my parts to be shipped. This was fine by me as I got to have unlimited popsicles. Since I was in the pediatric unit I could watch new VHS movies from Disney on a big TV cart that the nurses would roll in. They also had different gaming systems so I played Nintendo and Super NES which, until then, I had only heard about!

Waking up from the real surgery was NOT easy peasy. I remember being stirred in the operating room and told very loudly to wake up and that everything went well. Then they said to take a deep breath and blow out hard. If I knew what feeling and throat issues would happen after those commands I would have never done it. Uffda. Even as I write these words I can feel those same feelings of something being ripped out of my throat, fear of not being able to breathe, and the sensation of knives cutting my trachea with every breath. In the recovery room there was more loud talking at me. I began to wince in pain and have anxiety as I thought there was a boa constrictor on my arm. I woke up real fast. I remember the nurse looking at me intently over the bed rail when she figured out I wasn't hallucinating about a snake, that it was the painfully tight blood pressure cuff hurting my arm. She just giggled at me and calmed my fears by showing me my arm. No snake, just a stupid, pain-creating cuff. As I came in and out of sleepiness I had another rude awakening. I couldn't move my left knee, but it was my right knee they were supposed to hack open. Did they do the wrong leg?!? The nurse uncovered my legs to show me my left knee was just in a very long and thick wrap to make sure I don't hurt that fragile femur fracture as I heal from the new knee replacement on the right. Thanks to the TV show *20/20* for showing me all the horribly scary surgery stories of people having the wrong appendage amputated or the wrong organ taken out.

Knee replacements and their recovery/rehab are no joke. The pain and swelling disable you more than pre-surgery pain. I am ever thankful that the Lord collects our tears in His bottle and He removes many hard memories from our brains.

My other memory was being post surgical in biology class where we were in a lab setting. Lab tables are by design not wheelchair friendly, so I had a small table at the front of the room by the door. I could have one friend sit with me to be my lab partner. On this particular day I got two more friends to join me, unexpectedly. I had just taken my pain medicine because the pain from the morning bus ride was unbearable. So in the middle of a lecture I had to pop my pills. A few minutes later I had my lab partner friend sitting next to me pushing on my shoulder. I guess my meds were kicking in and I was starting to lean over out of my chair so she was holding me up. Then moments later another friend appeared sitting on my other side with their hand on my shoulder as I was trying to lean out of that side.

And before I knew it I had a third friend sitting in front of me knee to knee because I had started to slide out of my chair since the side escapes were being blocked. My high school friends still bring up this memory from time to time because they were so concerned, and also because it was very funny. I remember parts of this story from a very groggy state of mind and who knows what I was saying to them as they helped me. I assume somehow I got down to the nurse's office or was brought home...those details are unknown. Real friends keep you in your wheelchair!

Chapter 5

Jenna Jail

"Do Not Pass Go. Do Not Collect $200."
- Monopoly

When I was 16 I got my first job at our after school and summer latchkey program for elementary students. I only received this job because the county helped the school district pay my wage through a starting to work program due to my disability. I didn't really know how it all worked. I was just excited to earn some money and do it while playing games, doing crafts, and playing outdoors with younger students. I learned how to play lots of games that I didn't play as a child like Candyland, Mancala, Chutes and Ladders, Chess, and Guess Who? One summer I had little mini lessons with some of Fitz's summer band students while I was working. I really didn't know what I was doing, but playing music and getting paid for it instead of being out on the hot asphalt playground with no shade was fine by me. I had a fun little kid named Casey who was my main shadow while I worked. He always loved pushing me and getting put in Jenna jail! He was never in trouble, but when we would be in the gym he would go up against the wall and then I would back my chair up to the wall trapping him. He was so skinny, flexible, and strong that he could either push himself up using my handlebars to get his legs over one of my back wheels to escape, or his favorite was bending down so he could crawl out under my chair. Another trust game he loved to play was laying flat on the ground and having his arms on his body so I could literally run him over the long way. Other kids wanted to try and it quickly built trust and fun between us all. There was another little girl who didn't say much, but she would climb up on my lap and she was my shadow on days when Casey wasn't there. The cool thing with this job was that kids younger than me got to be around someone in a wheelchair, and they learned the do's and don'ts of engaging with someone in a chair. They also learned to see me beyond my wheelchair and they also developed more empathy.

One day I was out on the playground playing in the hot sun with the kids and thought I was shooing a fly away behind my knee but it ended up being a hornet that stung me. This was not a fun memory for me but seeing all the kids become so concerned for me was heartwarming. After a bit of being inside with an ice pack on we quickly went back outside with kids taking turns jumping on my back pegs and running and riding my chair around the safe parts of the playground. Because they were so small and light they could get my chair going faster and longer than my high school friends at lunch time. My only scary time and more adult time during my role here was when I was the "adult" inside near closing time and a child outside had fallen from the monkey bars. He was walking on them in an unsafe way and he fell and horribly broke his arm. Since I was the only one inside at the time I got to call 911 and be the radio go between the 911 operator and our boss out with the student. This memory will forever stick with me but it also prepared me for the many times of needing to call 911 for a host of different reasons and non-emergent needs as well.

I went on to have another three surgeries during my high school career. I had my other knee replaced, my right hip replaced, and my hamstrings and heel cords lengthened, which is the surgery my pediatric orthopedic surgeon was the lead on. It was during my hospital stay after the heel cord surgery that my surgeon, Dr. Gordon, came to do his rounds late at night. I was watching a movie called *Inner Space* which was a medical story of a doctor getting shrunk so he could be microscopic and be injected into his patient's body. When Dr. Gordon came into the room the doctor was exploring the internal organs. He started to gag and asked what in the world I was watching. I laughed so hard. I was like, "You just were inside my body fixing things and this grosses you out?" He said, "Oh no blood and organs are not my thing. I like bones and being a carpenter!" This is such a vivid memory.

I only have a few memories after this surgery, which include being back in school and having Fitz help me tighten my knee braces in her band office before or during high school band rehearsals. I had to have special foot plate attachments put on my wheelchair so my legs could be out straight in front of me. Oh, that was so painful on my hips, bum, and back. I also hated riding the school bus as every crack in the road caused sharp pains. Our rural roads don't just have cracks, we have big potholes and chuck holes. I got used to seeing teary eyes in all the adults around me because they did not like seeing me cry or having me hum, growl, or cry out in pain when those bad bumps happened. I don't know what was worse, my physical pain or seeing the emotional pain it caused for others. It was all just brutal.

Chapter 6

Standing Hugs Only

"I have learned that every day you should reach out and touch someone." - Maya Angelou

Like many of us, high school had its ups and downs for me. Most of my memories are positive and full of rich friendships. Many memories revolve around my activities and interests such as friends, band, jazz band, pep band, the school newspaper, pep club, National Honor Society, and lots of shenanigans.

My life made me mature very quickly. While life can be very serious and hard, I choose to embrace times when I can be silly, weird, and a bit out of my norm. In high school it was being late for class and being excused blaming the antiquated freight elevator that had a pull gate door.

If previous users didn't get the gate door all the way closed, then you had to "borrow someone's legs" to go check the other two floors to close the gate so the elevator would work. My friends and I may have used that excuse successfully a few times to get out of a tardy. Sorry teachers!

Also, in high school my good friends would go out to off campus lunch with me on nice weather days. Our old high school was on a large hill in a downtown neighborhood. Getting out the back alley to the road was treacherous most times, but the freedom of the hills provided many scary and fun adventures. My friends would run to give me more momentum and then jump on the back of my chair where I had two little posts coming out of my frame for my anti-tip bars. I had to have my feet plate on and scoot forward in my chair a little so I could counterbalance their added weight. A few of my friends were too tall, so giving them a ride was scary or impossible. The main part of our high school hill that we could ride is about a half of a block long but pretty steep. It is a sideroad leading to the school bus garage, Hardees, a fast food restaurant, Hwy 61, and a gas station. The road flattens out down by the bus garage, but then immediately has a climb up to the highway and to the gas station. Our goal during one season of adventure was to time it just right so we would go careening down high school hill and get a green light over the highway to get to the gas station without my friend having to jump off. It took us many trials and errors to finally accomplish this...once. The freedom, laughter, and bond built in trust during these times is indescribable.

During special times of life I wanted to show my dear friends my appreciation for their care and love for me. Usually people show this through hugs. As an eyeglass wearer I always get the standing person's shoulder right in the glasses, which does not feel good. So I wanted to figure out other options as well as show off my new found tricks thanks to Sue, my Physical Therapist (PT), who helped me learn how to give a standing hug. I will never forget my first attempt having to stand up without assistance and both my arms ended up on her shoulders like a middle school boy dancing with a girl, or like Frankenstein being propped up by another human. She was laughing so hard and teasing me about my lack of knowing how to hug. We eventually figured it out, but man standing hugs need a LOT of balance! Sometimes my standing hugs can be more awkward than seated hugs to a standing person. Now I have taught my dear friends how to have seated hugs so we can both be on equal footing, and both enjoy the hug instead of being hurt or awkward.

Fitz and I, 1997.

Since I knew that I wanted to be a middle school band director since sophomore year of high school, I started taking summer lessons from Fitz on all the different instruments of the band world. She helped me figure out which ones would be my main instruments in each family and which ones would need many adaptations for my right fused elbow, my "hook." We had fun and I remember lots of laughs as we attempted different accommodations. I also started piano lessons with a local teacher during the school year so I could play piano a little with my left hand. My primary goal was understanding the piano and basic music theory. Music was my passion and became an integral part of my everyday life and identity.

I had to defer my driver license a few years due to needed surgeries when I was 16 and 17. I took the classwork with my peers but my behind the wheel time had to wait a bit. In order for someone with a disability to take the behind the wheel portion, you had to be assessed by a mobility driving specialist. I had to go to Duluth to Polinsky Rehab to meet this specialist. Everything was fine in the physical assessment and I knew I would be using my legs to drive and not hand controls, but I had to prove this...in a car, in a big city with huge hills, on busy medical campus streets, having never driven a car before. Yeah, it was scary beyond words. To make matters worse, halfway through the driving trial they made me use hand controls. To be alive to share this story is a feat in itself. My brain was in fight or flight mode even hours after this experience, and my friends couldn't believe I drove in Duluth for my first time driving. I was cleared to start my behind the wheel course, and from what I remember that went fine until we had our final drive to and around Duluth, which is the final trip of the course. My mom came along as a back seat driver. We were downtown where there are a lot of different one way streets. I was VERY familiar with all the streets and their directions due to our medical trips at least three days a week. We got to a familiar corner and my instructor told me to turn left and that this road is a one way so I needed to turn a hard left. I knew this was a two way but I did not know how to voice up to my instructor. This was a hard call as I knew what was right and legal, but I also wanted to follow my teacher's instruction and not fail my class. I also did not want to kill anyone that day. So I did the legal move and ignored my instructor. After the turn was complete he thanked me for ignoring his directions and profusely apologized to my mom and me. These experiences still baffle me, that you would have someone with a mobility disability break the law in getting behind a wheel to drive unlicensed to prove they can get a license. *I hope these practices and systems have changed!*

I got to take my new-to-me car to graduation! I had not had time to get my car adapted with my wheelchair topper, so I always needed friends or family with me to fold and store my chair in the trunk. My friend rode with me to graduation. This was an evening filled with emotions and excitement. I was speaking and sharing my life: the good and bad of growing up in our town and all the challenges I and our community faced. But also I was walking in the procession and across the stage! I had worked for months with my health teacher.

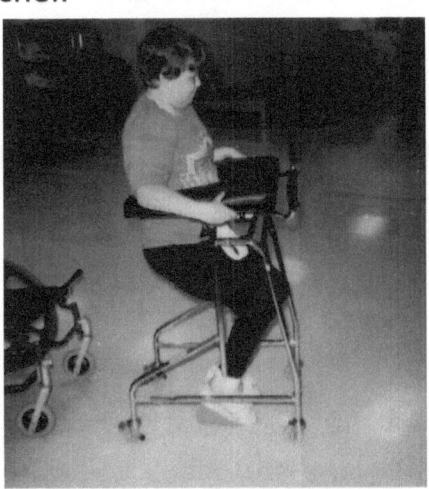

My "Magic Shoes" and "Evil" (Eva) Walker, early 1990's before all my joint replacement surgeries.

I had started by using an Eva Walker, which I called the Evil Walker because it had caused such pain and fatigue for me. It is a platform walker so I could lean on my elbows for support, instead of typical walkers where you load your weight through your hands and wrists. I also wore my "magic shoes" and braces. My magic shoes were coined from *Forrest Gump* because without these tennis shoes, that had built up angled wedges which compensated for my ankles not flexing, I was unable to stand AND walk. Picture Barbie trying to walk on her toes; this was the condition of my ankles, but once we built the ground up to my heels I could balance and walk without as much pain.

My health teacher was a determined soul and she raised the bar for everyone around her. When she caught wind that I wanted to walk for graduation, she gave up many lunches and preps each week to torture me, I mean, to encourage me to make this goal a reality. Between her sacrifice and dedication as well as my PTs, I went from using a walker to Lofstrand crutches, the type that have a cuff on your forearm. We built up the handles so my straight wrists could hold the handle without slipping off or causing wrist and hand damage. We also got me walking stairs as the graduation stage was not wheelchair accessible, so I had to go up and down about four steps on each side of the stage. Once I got steady on my feet I not only had to work with my teacher, but also my friends who were walking with me. My friend, who was my walking partner, helped me navigate the stairs in a gown with extra flowy parts that could have easily caused a fall.

Earlier that day I had lunch with Fitz on the auditorium stage and I blurted out about me speaking that night. She originally wasn't coming to graduation, but this changed after I told her I was speaking and walking. After all, she was a part of my graduation speech as she was a pivotal teacher in my life who saw me as a human and inspired me to continue my education to become a middle school band teacher. I will always remember being a quarter of the way through my processional walk and seeing her and hearing her yell, "You go, girl!" I remember hugging my dad and mom after my speech, which was a big deal as my family are not huggers to show love but more teasers to show love. I ended my speech with the poem *Don't Quit,* from a treasured surgery gift. And I will always remember my civics teacher, Mr. Swanstrom, starting the standing ovation as I crossed the stage and received my diploma. It was a miracle I didn't fall and crush my friend on the way down the stairs with my tearfilled eyes.

"You Go, girl!" at Graduation, 1998.

Don't Quit Poem- Unknown- abridged version
as read at 1998 high school graduation

Don't Quit

When things go wrong as they sometimes will,
When the road you're trudging seems all uphill,
When funds are low and debts are high,
And you want to smile but you have to sigh,
When care is pressing you down a bit,
Rest if you must, but don't you quit.

Life is strange with its twists and turns,
As everyone of us sometimes learns,
And many a failure turns about
When we might have won had we stuck it out,
Don't give up though the pace seems slow,
You may succeed with another blow.

Success is failure turned inside out,
The silver lining of the clouds of doubt,
And you never can tell how close you are-
It may be near when it seems so far.
So stick to the fight when you are hardest hit,
It's when things seem worst that you
MUST NOT QUIT!

And then a surprise occurred right after the ceremony in the front lawn of the school. My former PT , the one who taught me to hug, had come back to see me walk across the stage. She had left for her next chapter of life and marriage right in the middle of my walking and stair climbing process. She experienced my one and only fall in PT as she was training in my new PT, Diane. She was a true Physical Torturer and had me walk a long distance before climbing down a flight of stairs. When I got to the landing between the flight, I told her my legs were ready to give out but she pushed me to continue, even though I knew I should have listened to my body. Two steps into going down the second set of steps I just sat down. All three of us were scared and did not expect my body to react this way. We were laughing so hard from being so shocked and scared. Diane went running for my wheelchair that was back out in the hospital area and carried it down the stairs. But we knew I just had to rest and I had to walk the rest of the flight cause there was no other way out of this pickle. Diane still treats me today, and we still laugh and shake our heads at this memory.

My favorite pictures from graduation are of friends and family, of my dad hugging me, and of my surprise medical team with my former PT sitting on my lap. It is the relationships that make our memories and life celebrations more meaningful. It is these long term and short term interactions with fellow humans that make us or break us. It is the sacrifice of teachers to go above and beyond their call of duty to clear the path of obstacles for their students, which impacts their direction for the rest of their lives.

After my high school graduation Jaime and I made the trip to Decorah, Iowa, to see Lisa! In our eclectic style, we kept Jaime as the surprise and we also had fun dressing up like Pauly Shore in *Son In Law* (*if you don't know this movie— look it up*). This was a hilarious movie the three of us had watched in the theater together and we still reference our groovy memories of that time together. By this time Lisa's family had grown to two children, and we had an amazing time making a beautiful old farm house work for us in our chairs. We got to meet Lisa's parents and her Nigerian brother. It was the beginning of being family.

Jaime, Lisa, and I, Iowa, 1999.

Chapter 7

Shenanigan University

"Education is the most powerful weapon which you can use to change the world." - Nelson Mandela

I would have not passed my freshman music theory at the local university in Duluth if it wasn't for my piano lessons in high school. During my college days I went back home in the early summers to help the new high school band director with summer band lessons, and during the school year to run private trumpet lessons and sectionals. It was always a fun trip and I loved working with hard working young trumpet players. Their drive always reinspired my love of music and playing the trumpet.

During my freshman and sophomore years of college, I lived in the dorms as the university buildings were all connected by indoor skywalks and tunnels. This was one of the deciding factors for choosing the university over other colleges, since the winters would be especially hard to navigate independently. In our region we can see an annual average of 81 inches of snow and many weeks of below zero temperatures. Snow and ice removal are very inconsistent so I must always have help when outdoors. There was also an amazing trumpet professor who always clicked with me when I would play for him at high school contests. Unfortunately, the summer before I started college, this professor retired.

Dorm life was interesting to start off with. We had bunk beds in our little dorm, so of course my roommate got the top bunk. We barely lasted a quarter together as my needs for a clean floor and her method of laundry and clothes keeping did not match up. I felt bad that things had gotten so tense between us, but thankfully the housing department worked with us. After some time we could still be friends and hang with our mutual friends. We realized we just weren't meant to live together and that was ok. I struggled with finding words to describe my needs and to set healthy boundaries. Part of this was being away from home for the first time and all the things one learns about themselves, the world, and others in this pivotal year of life. We had a great hallway of freshman girls to learn with and from. What happens freshman year stays in freshman year, but there were plenty of exhausting and hilarious late nights: at Perkins thanks to fire alarms going off, fun movie and TV nights, and deepening friendships that grew through conversations over misconceptions or false teachings of different religions, cultures, and assumptions from our home lives and times of growing up.

I also had a dorm neighbor who had JRA. She was still walking and had more neck fusion and finger contractures. We were good neighbors, but then we had a conversation one day and it became very apparent that I was the poster child of what she never wanted to become. I wish I could say that we were mature and talked through this, living out our Christian values, but we did not. But let's be honest, college freshmen can't handle these big hurts and life questions with grace and forgiveness. For me this was a weird new phase as so many from non-disabled culture always made me out to be this inspirational story, one with courage they hoped they would have to face their own adversity. So this was the first time I was ever confronted with pity and being despised for who I had become. I thought she would be an ally because of our shared experience. But instead I became her inspiration of going to work-out, eating right, and doing all these things so she "doesn't become like me." #ouch

The schedule of a music education major was grueling. 8 AM classes every day continueds straight through until sometimes 5—7 PM fol-lowed by additional rehearsals, practice time, or concerts you were playing in, helping at, or attend-ing for required class work. We had many classes for zero or half credits, so when other majors complained about having 5 classes in a quarter and I had over 15 classes, I had no pity for them. But these grueling hours and commitments did prepare me very well for my career, and just life in general. Some of my deepest connections hap-pened in the late nights in the practice rooms, or on road trips to meet family or friends or when our ensemble went on tour. There may or may not have been a time at the state music educators' conference when we piled seven people into my Grand Prix in downtown Minneapolis so we could get to a local music store during our break between practice and performance. One of the seven may or may not have also been one of our professors, and we may have driven by a few cop cars. The things I have gotten talked into over the years for the sake of fun and to be "one of the guys"...Uffda.

My first "real" job without county help started during my sophomore year in college at Schmitt Music. I was a contracted lesson teacher of all band instruments, beginning strings (if needed), and voice. I worked here for several years, and on many days I spent my earnings at Barnes and Noble or on a meal, as many students would be no call-no shows. I learned a lot about the music retail business and made very good friendships with the music retailers, my boss, and other studio teachers. This experience was also invaluable as I learned about other local school band programs, and the wide variety of band lesson books which were used at each school. I also experienced tips, tricks, and strategies other band teachers used to inspire their students.

When I think back to these college days and all the hauling of instruments plus getting through snow and ice just to get to work, it makes me exhausted and beyond blessed to think about all the work and dedication I had in those young days.

I attended an Arthritis Foundation event where the speaker was a middle aged woman and mom with JRA. Her story and insights were life changing for me. She worked for the local hospital as the "voice of the hospital." You heard her on all the recordings in all the departments. This was the first time I had ever thought about my voice being my career after my hands and other joints impede my work as a music educator. She also was very candid about pregnancy and how her JRA was amazing during pregnancy, but as soon as she gave birth she went into a tailspin of flare ups. Even though I never had children, this stuck with me and I got to share this with my youth group student after she had her twins. I wish I had known to share all of this with her in advance, as her doctors did not prepare her or her medical plan for this huge fallout after giving birth.

During my college days I had multiple surgeries. Many times my body hadn't fully healed before having the next surgery. I had my ankles replaced, my knees and hip replacements revised, and one of my hardest surgeries—my left elbow replaced. Remember, my right elbow has been fused nearly straight since age 12, so even though I wrote right handed everything else was completed by my left hand. For this elbow replacement I had to have my first picc line, which is like a two-way IV but in the neck. Ouch! I felt the most disabled in all my life during this surgical rehab because neither hand could reach my face. I relied on others to feed me, give me my pills and drink, and even pick my nose! These were hard and tear-filled weeks. When people are helping you do everything it is humbling, annoying, frustrating, trust and bond building quicker than anything else.

Chapter 8

More Than Just My Wheels

"I simply refused to accept what I was told about who I could be." - Judith Heumann

One of my greatest trips to Iowa was a solo trip. I only took a couple of these trips as I needed more help with daily living tasks, such as dressing and overcoming the lack of accessible wheel-in showers in hotels. Most showers have the bench on one side and the handheld shower six to ten feet across the shower on the opposing wall, which is definitely not usable independently, or safe. The trip across Minnesota and then into Iowa takes five hours. In that time I need help pumping gas and maybe in gas station restrooms if the floors are wet or slippery.

On one of these beautiful solo summer trips I stopped to see Fitz in Albert Lea. My heart was full from seeing my dear friend and catching up with her. I was on a new tour of southern Minnesota when I came across a detour. Normally I would have freaked out because this was well before GPS on cell phones. I was reading maps and trying to get safely to Decorah on roads I had never traveled. Instead, I had a peace that passed all understanding, so I trusted the detour signs. Being down in farm country, I lost my radio signal. I usually listened to classic rock, classical, jazz or RnB, but on this detour I just kept hitting the scan button on the radio. I came across a Christian radio station and gave it a chance. I was in college at this time as a music ed major, so many times I was so overwhelmed with music that I just liked the quiet. Many times during the detour I turned off the radio to just enjoy the sunshine, heat, and wind in my hair. But I kept being drawn back to the radio. My music listening changed forever that day and I remember it fondly. This day led to me eventually playing trumpet and singing on several church worship teams, and really the cultivation of my heart for worship. Throughout college

I had experiences of being a church musician on Easter and Christmas as a trumpet player, but I was always left with an empty heart after those paid "gigs." My heart changed and my choices of how and when I use these musical talents also shifted. There is something so deep and personal in our music as we lift up our spirits to the One who created them. Our voice is so personal and vulnerable as each voice is specific and unique to each person they live in. Teaching my students to use their voice or instrument was one of my greatest joys and humblest of callings. *Thinking back on all the ways this one detour impacted my life leaves me awestruck.*

During my junior year of college I took the plunge and moved off campus with my dear friend Jaime, to the west side of town. We lived in an accessible townhome. It was very nice as Jaime got to use the garage, and I had my own accessible parking spot near our dumpster. We had a little sidewalk ramp that led to our grassy yard. It was nice putting my toes and feet on the fresh grass, especially after my ankle surgeries. After your feet are stuck in casts for several months the whole world is a sensory playground.

This little ramp also served another important memory on September 12, 2001. It is where we lined up our candles each night in remembrance of lives lost and our country mourning the terror attacks of 9/11. I will always remember this day, not just for the common reasons we all share as Americans, but also because Jaime was up in a plane that day during the attacks. We had no idea if she was ok or where her plane was. She came home safely from this trip, which was supposed to be one of her usual adventures around the US, but it had a very different memory attached to it. Even though we only lived in that place for a year it holds many memories of cooking together, laughter, tears, celebrations, and heartache. I had a surgery or two while we lived there. I lost my grandma and one of my great aunts as well as an uncle. It was a VERY hard year for my family, but living with Jaime taught me a lot about life and weathering the storms it brings to each of us. When I look back at this time, I marvel at all the things I was physically able to do. Even though we say it was an accessible place, there were many things that were not. Like, we could have easily fallen into our oven as we had to open the door from the side, and dear Jaime could have easily fallen into our top loading washer as she had to stand and lunge herself over the tall front wall of the machine to reach the clothes in the bottom. If she threw herself too hard or high, she could have landed head first in the washing machine. Jaime always teaches me about life just by being herself. There is no greater gift than being in someone's day to day life. We could write our own book on our adventures together, but we could end up in some trouble if those adventures met the page. That year of sharing an accessible townhome was filled with fun and heartache, adventure and surgery. I have no idea how I got out to my car and removed snow each and every day; oh wait, yes I do, my dear music friend.

She lived just a few townhomes away and would walk to our townhome every school morning. This dear music friend was a piano pedagogy major who was a loyal friend, a straight talker, open to people different from herself, and an atheist willing to discuss hard topics. She opened my eyes to other perspectives of life and to a much broader world of music. She liked lots of 21st century composers, prepared piano, and loathed the music I listened to like Christian and popular Baroque music. She called herself my sherpa as she carried my numerous instruments and bags. She did snow removal and helped with my wheelchair when my car topper wouldn't work, or if my conversion vehicle had to be in the shop. My friend had her license but did not drive. So our friendship was a great one of give and take for each other. She was a piano pedagogy major and I was a music ed major, so some of our classes were the same but many were not. She got many extra hours of practice each week as she waited for me to finish all of my rehearsals and classes. Slowly our worlds drifted apart, but we are still friends on social media and help each other out when it is needed. She ended up marrying our freshman music theory professor and has a child, and I am single and childless. I only share this as it is funny how life changes from our college ideals and dreams. If you went back to talk to our college selves she would have said she would maybe have married but definitely no kids, and I would have said I would absolutely be married and maybe have kids, if the Lord allowed. I am very happy for her and am ecstatic that life had other paths for her as she is a great wife and mother. I am beyond thankful for our long and hard discussions, as she challenged me to think and know why I believe what I believe. Also, people can be friends and share life with others who are very different from themselves.

Jaime ended up taking a job in Indiana before our lease was up, so I actually lived in our townhome alone for the last several months. I was very thankful my loyal friend was near, but having the townhouse to myself was kind of eerie at times. I missed the vibrancy Jaime brought to our home and also her fun friends from disability culture. I remember once her friend, our former wheelchair basketball coach, came over for dinner and a movie. He was a funny guy who could do all those two wheeled dance moves in his lightweight sports chair. I will always remember him popping a wheelie to watch the movie and he propped the back of his chair on our pretty low couch. His upper body and core strength still leave me in awe today.

Jaime and I also had a cute elderly couple as our neighbors who would keep tabs on us. They were always kind and sitting out on their porch when the weather allowed.

I found another apartment more centrally located in Duluth and closer to my college. It was not as large or accessible, but it had its good points and younger landlords that could better help with projects and snow removal. It had a fun little cement patio as my access to my apartment while all the other apartments had a security door that was up some stairs, but I had a "hidden" entrance to the side of the stairs. I loved sitting out there reading, and even had a few pots for plants in the summers. Funny thing is my piano pedagogy friend moved to a building just down the street, and another trumpet buddy and his girlfriend also moved into the other building down the way.

My trumpet buddy, Brian, is a funny guy. He has lots of nicknames and always has a name for me. He is a smart tech guy and is big into gear for his trumpets and his audio gigs. One night he and his girlfriend, now wife, came up for some dinner and games. It was a pretty run of the mill time together having fun and joking while they taught me California Rummy. Well things got weird when

Brian ran to the restroom. His girlfriend just came out and asked me if I had any romantic feelings for him as she was willing to "fight me for him." I think I probably couldn't keep my face from showing disgust and hilarity all at once. I mean, Brian is a great guy BUT he is my trumpet brother so it was like thinking of kissing your brother, and then hilarious to me that this non-disabled cute blonde was threatened by me, a chick in a chair who was not looking for a relationship at that time cause life was hard enough with all my medical junk. *I still look back on that night and just laugh!*

Since this new apartment had a sliding glass door, it took no time at all to hurt my upper back and arms. Eventually my landlords changed it out for a nice metal security door, which was way more accessible, but I did miss my screen door on those hot summer days. During this time I needed more surgeries and needed more help around the house with activities, such as housekeeping, grocery shopping, and basic meal prep so I would not be forced to eat fast food, delivery or frozen meals. I was connected with the county and received my first Community Access for Disability Inclusion (CADI) Waiver. A CADI Waiver brings resources and funds into your life to help cover disability and accommodation expenses. My first new level of assistance was the CADI providing a homemaker. It was weird letting complete strangers enter my home to help me with food prep, errands, and housekeeping. Learning the new systems of what we could do and could not do was a steep learning curve. Homemaking did not require any type of training, so all of those skills fell to me to teach these nice but random ladies how I needed things done. This was also a very low paying job and my first homemaker had no vehicle. She had to use the public transit which did not have any good local bus stops, as my apartment was on a steep hill and her home was on the far west side of town. I eventually got in trouble with the company for transporting her to and from work. I knew that probably wasn't the right thing to do as she was supposed to be in my life to help me, not add more work and expense to me. However, she was my only option for help, so driving her both ways once a week seemed like the least I could do to get work done that I could not physically do alone.

During this time I also started getting Personal Care Assistance (PCA), which brought d more random ladies in and out of my life. Some were amazing, open, honest, and fun while others were not. Opening one's life and personal cares to complete strangers is daunting, vulnerable, and many times frustrating and exhausting. I worked with a local company to get help each morning and evening. They were extremely frustrated by my early morning schedule needs so I could be at college by 8 AM, and then needing help again at night before bed for therapies and home care. The company wanted me to have the same schedule everyday to make their lives easier, not to truly make my life manageable and fulfilled while being a productive member of society. (I wish I could say that this mindset has changed greatly but it has only changed minimally, in my experience and opinion.) Thankfully my parents, family, college friends, and some church family members lived and worked relatively close to my new apartment, so when PCAs didn't show they could sometimes come and help me.

I need help on a regular basis with minimal dressing needs, some grooming assistance since

I only have one hand that can touch my head and neck, as well as food prep with lifting, cutting, and transferring dishes of food in and out of hot, inaccessible ovens. I also need help with housekeeping and grocery shopping, as repetitive motions and lifting or carrying items of certain weights is hurtful to my already sore joints. Imagine your morning routine and choose one thing you can no longer do yourself. Think of all the words and demonstrations you would need to give someone to attempt to do this for you. You and your helper would soon figure out that your left isn't their left, and your version of gentle is not their version of gentle. Just this one task that took you seconds independently would now take many minutes or more with the help of others. Now, picture not just one thing needing help but half or all of your morning routine...time consuming, exhausting, and frustrating!

During this season of life I also needed dental surgery to remove my wisdom teeth, and an adult front tooth that was crowded out so it grew behind my front teeth. As a trumpet player playing at the college level as a music major, this surgery and recovery caused many issues as I had to learn how to play all over again. This tooth was where I had learned to stop my tongue which created every note I had ever played. Being in your 20's and relearning what you learned at age 12 was overwhelmingly hard. This issue happened because, as a child with JRA, my lower jaw had stunted growth. Technically, I was supposed to have oral surgery when I was younger to make more room for my adult teeth, but this involved breaking my jaw and wiring it shut. My rheumatologist vetoed this surgery as there was no promise that my arthritis would not fuse my jaw. I could live with an overbite and the ridges on my bottom teeth being there forever, but having issues speaking and eating would have just been too much added to all my other medical issues.

As many times as there were great memories, there were also hard and hurtful memories. I was in college from 1998—2003, which was 8—13 years after the Americans with DIsabilities Act (ADA) was passed into law. The ADA protected the rights of people with disabilities to have equal access to spaces, education, work, and everyday life that could not be discriminated against due to medical or physical needs. Music wasn't the crown jewel of the university's campus, thus we had random practice spaces where they would give us space. Our main instrumental rehearsal space was in a large room under the theater department. I had to go through the black box theater which could have all sorts of obstacles and hazards like nails and screws all over, which several times popped my tires on the way to class. I then took a freight elevator ride to the lower level, and if the elevator was out of order or if I was unable to use it due to theater needs, I would have to ride the front areas of the stage which would go up and down with the help of the shop employee. As if dealing with these physical issues was not enough, I also had to deal with the attitudes of old professors that had no idea the amount of work I went through to make it to their class on time— which was late to them, or a few minutes late, which was like death to them. Oh, and not to mention that if I had to use the restroom that was accessible, I had to navigate all of these issues again to then go into an adjacent building, while my non-disabled peers could just go down the hall in the same building for their restroom needs.

There were many attitudinal barriers I faced from my peers and some professors. I had many accommodations from other lesson instructors and classroom teachers because some professors simply could not handle the fact that I had to play instruments in other ways, like putting a violin on my knee and playing it like a cello. (Please check out Gaelynn Lea Music as she has made this style of violin playing her career and amazing talent— www.violinscratches.com) I was once in the thick of so many discrimination issues that my new trumpet teacher and I had a heart to heart, and he finally asked me the hard question, "Do you feel like Job, right now?" Even in my limited Bible knowledge at that time of my faith walk I knew I was nowhere near Job status, but I could see where my teacher could find similarities. Every area of my college track looked bleak, not because of my lack of ability, dedication, or call-ing to this career, but simply because some adults and elders could not get over my wheelchair or lack of hand dexterity.

I was the split lead trumpet player in Jazz II and since there were no ramps to the jazz risers, my trumpet brothers and few sisters would have to learn how to lift me in my wheelchair up the two risers. The near falls and funny shenanigans we had to do to make music work for me was inhumane and intense. My senior year at our biggest jazz concert I used my new powerchair that I got for conducting and jazz lead trumpet playing. Well, the guys had a heck of a time lifting this even heavier chair with me in it. At the end of the amazing show, we took the stage with Jazz I and played our closing song of *Sing! Sing! Sing!* It was smoking! And after the crowd cleared, so was I! The powerchair had started to smoke as I had stretched the cable during my elevation stage for playing, and the motor could not get it to go back down. My trumpet brothers and bandmates had to help me down from my smoking powerchair, back into my everyday wheels, and then haul the heavy chair down off the risers. Once we got the tension off of the overextended cable, the chair was able to go back to its regular height and drive to its storage area where it awaited repair.

My desire to be a music educator wasn't to be the most flashy teacher or know the most music theory, but to show how music can be a lifesaver like it had been for me all these years. I knew

I preferred a rural setting as many rural schools can only hire one music teacher, so I wanted to get my vocal music education degree for K—12 in addition to my Instrumental degree. Due to my arthritis, I knew my hands could really be the next body part to be sabotaged, so I wanted my voice to be confident and strong. I had sung my whole life with my oldest sister around the house, and at this point in college I started singing on a worship team at church. Of course I had hoops to jump through to add a major, and many more attitudinal barriers. My definition of attitudinal barriers is when others make assumptions or have unconscious biases towards me based on my wheels and not on me— the human sitting in the wheels. An example of this is when I was out for lunch with a friend in the middle of winter. She was trying to push me through the snowy parking lot when a worker yelled across the way asking if she could help her with THAT. This stranger never talked to me, looked at me, or acknowledged my human existence. Many times I am an inanimate object in peoples' words and actions. People can create tension, more work, or create more barriers with their attitudes and treatment of me because they are unwilling to see life from another perspective, usually a seated one. A great example of this is, where I live, they put all postings at six feet or higher on walls. This is unrealistic for standing people to all read let alone those wheeling through life at 4' 2". When you take away barriers for disabled people, you tend to take away barriers for many other people groups, too.

An example of an attitudinal barrier is when the head of the vocal department did not want me to get this second degree. While I can understand some of their concerns, they didn't really know me or my plans. They also did not know that I would not accept jobs I could not physically do in a modified way. After many meetings with music department leaders and my advisor, who was the head of the music department, we came to an agreement on the classes and student teaching I needed for the vocal degree after my instrumental degree was complete.

I was so excited to finish my student teaching for band, work over the summer on my new degree, and then come back refreshed to start my additional degree. However, that excitement quickly got burned up like the chaff as I had my end of student teaching meeting with my cooperating teacher and my collegiate musical father figure. Both of them in their own terms told me, "I hope you find your passion, and maybe we will see you back here to get your special ed license as we think you could do amazing work there."

I was stunned by their ableism. This was such a blow to my heart. They were role models I looked up to. Did they really not see my passion and abilities to bridge the gaps and bring music to all students at all ability levels? Had they put me in a small box in their minds that disabled can only teach the disabled? These words cut very deep and left me wounded for a long time.

Chapter 9

My Heart is Home

"Home is where the heart is." - Unknown

I began having yearly trips to Decorah, Iowa, and watched Lisa's family grow to five kids! Some of the trips early on I did solo, but as my disease progressed and I began needing daily help, I had the pleasure of bringing friends and PCAs with me to meet my Iowa Family and my home away from home. The small college town made an impact on my heart, and for me there is just a peace in my heart when I drive over the hill and see the beginning of the town. My eyes well up as I climb that hill each time, and my floodgates break free when I am climbing that hill again saying, "See ya later."

My Iowa family created a special place by just being them, and by creating a safe place for me to thrive, heal, and figure out who I am and what I am created to be and do. I am a part of their everyday life when I am there, and now thanks to technology, I am a part of the three older kids' lives in pretty cool, deep, and God-honoring ways. They all definitely have my heart as a family and individually, too. My trips were always fun just tagging along to my friends' very busy lives as parents, business owners, and active church leaders. Dear Lisa is very much a Type B compared to my high strung Type A personality. Getting away from not following my overbooked schedule and just getting to be a tag along to watch and learn from her life of grace, love, and peace, even in the storms of crying kids, being late for events, and living out plan g instead of plan a, b, or c, was pure bliss to me. One time Lisa teased me saying there are other amazing places to visit and travel to instead of my annual trip to Decorah. I knew there were other places and adventures to explore, but I wasn't done learning and embracing what Decorah had to offer and why I felt at home here. It was just Jenna-friendly.

Jenna-friendly is a term I created to have shared vocabulary with friends, family, and peers. This means I can be safe in this space. It means I can accept a cup of coffee because I know I can wheel into an accessible bathroom for independent transfers with enough space for my chair next to the toilet, as well as access to easy use faucets, soap and towel dispensers. It also means glassware is light enough for me to lift and small enough for my hand to reach around to lift it, or a straw option is available. When in homes it means I have other seating options such as firmer couches or other chairs to transfer to and spaces at tables that I can pull up to for food, coffee, and my favorite...GAMES!

During my early years of Decorah visits I was able to stay at my Lisa's home. Their bathroom was not overly Jenna-friendly, so I would have to go to their PT business to shower and use their PT pool. As their kids grew and their house became more full as well as my physical needs changing, it became easier to stay at a local hotel. Through my trips I made some new friendships at this local hotel which was truly Jenna-friendly, both physically and attitudinally. I got to stay in all the different accessible rooms to finally find my favorite room. Early on I got to take their pool and hottub lifts for their maiden voyage and teach some of their new staff the ins and outs of helping folks with the lifts. I truly felt like I was coming home even to a hotel. Some of the local shop owners were just sweet gems remembering me from year to year, which included sweet conversations of what has happened in life since our last encounter. Decorah taught me about shopping locally and supporting the small businesses. Each trip I try to explore something new— a new part of their amazing paved trails, a new restaurant or shop, and a new food. Yes, Lisa even got me to try sushi! As my family teases me, if there is something new they want me to try, you get Jaime or Lisa to make me take the plunge.

I think we all need a Jaime, a Lisa, and a Decorah in our lives. I know my life is more full and blessed because of them all.

Lisa and I, 2013.

Chapter 10

Borrowing Arms and Legs

"I'm not Jenna. I'm just her legs." -DJ

I also was blessed to have some consistent PCAs who gave me dignity, true help, confidence, and laughter. Three of my first PCAs stand out as great helpers who were consistent, caring, and believed in me and my purposes in life. We shared many inside jokes and stories. We played many card or board games while I was in my standing frame to help keep my mind off the pain from being stretched from my back to my ankles. These ladies didn't just help me at home, but they also helped me at my first band teaching job at a private parochial elementary and middle school. My PCAs became my hands and feet in the music classroom, and they learned many skills a typical nursing student would never know, like how to tune a drum set or clean a trumpet. My students learned quickly that I borrow lots of arms and legs, especially in spaces that are less than "Jenna-friendly," aka accessible. Here, I taught in the gym-a-cafe-a-torium, the all stainless steel kitchen, and the band storage was under the stage, in the hall, and in the faculty bathroom!!! We had students climbing under the stage daily to get out stands, percussion, and anything else that fit under there. We had students setting up and tearing down whole band and jazz band set ups. Everyone had a job for themselves and for the band as a whole. We had lots of fun and grew an amazing little beginning and middle school program with the help of my dear PCAs. Building this band program was among the most fun aspects of my music teaching career. I started the Area Middle School Band Festival which followed me to my next school, then continued for over a decade due to the help of many friends and students.

Also during this time, I was blessed with a dear friend who taught fourth grade. We had many things in common such as faith, work ethic, and finding the bright side of the clouds life tends to bring our way. We had weekly lunches together in her welcoming classroom, which helped me feel like I belonged when much of the school was inaccessible to me. Besides my students, she was one of the hardest parts of the job to leave.

I handed my band program over to a new-to-the-area, veteran band director. The very day I accepted my new position in my hometown, I had received her promotional letter about her new music studio. I immediately called her asking for her to take over my band program. Talk about perfect timing! These were great next steps for each of us, and she went on to take this band program to the next level. It was so fun to come back and hear their concerts and cheer them all on!

Chapter 11

Hometown Adopted Grandmas

"Grandma's Rules"
If I'm home, you're always welcome.
If you're hungry, help yourself to anything.
If you break something, it's alright.
If you need anything, I'll buy it for you.
If you make a mess, help me clean it up.
When you leave, give lots of hugs and kisses.
Shared with me by Grandma "Pinky"

In public education, from my experience as a student and a teacher, there is a very false practice of pulling students with disabilities from their "non core" or elective classes to provide services. For me, as an elementary student, this happened during my music times...remember my failing of recorder class?

Fast forward fifteen years. I have returned to my hometown as a music teacher after achieving my double bachelors in instrumental and vocal music education. I left my parochial band teaching job to be in the public schools in my hometown at the new and fully accessible high school. Administration needed me to return to my elementary school to teach some general music and help out the full time teacher. Yup, you guessed it. This recorder class flunky was now a colleague to her recorder teacher! The Lord works in mysterious ways...

One of the great things about coming home to teach is having the great pleasure of reuniting with many kids from my latchkey job. My little shadow from seven years earlier was now our student director for the high school wind ensemble. From time to time, I would remind him of "Jenna jail" and we laughed and laughed. He is now a professional piano player. Memories made can provide much entertainment and healing in later days.

When I returned to my hometown to be a music educator, I joined a new church and became the youth director. Formally and mostly informally, I mentored several students with JRA. One youth group kid had a very similar story as Jaime, Nic, and myself. She and I are still in contact today, and help encourage each other over social media since we no longer live in the same town. Another student I remember had a different story. He was diagnosed later in childhood and was very active in hockey and other really physical activities. During this time Nic and I tried to start a JRA support group in Duluth, because we knew what a gift it was, as friends, to have helped each other through hard times. We wanted to help give that to our students and others, but the support group only met a few times as turnout was very limited. The new local pediatric rheumatologist shared that the medical model had changed; medications made kids "better" and prevented the huge joint losses Nic and I had. After this conversation, I really looked at a few of my students being treated with this new medical model, and things did look as the doctor described. Yet, I could still see the changes and hurt in the eyes of my students. They were experiencing something, but didn't yet have words to describe their pain, needs, or differences compared to more healthy peers and siblings.

I always had older friends, many who I "adopted" as parents or grandparents. My mom had similar friendships, which I think played a part in me developing these types of relationships. My medical journey also contributed, because I spent most of my waking hours with adult medical personnel who became my confidants and friends. I also had to grow up really fast, because at age 16 I was making life and death medical decisions regarding orthopedic surgeries and the course I wanted my life to take. I had lots of close friends in high school and college that were my own age, but my deepest friendships were with my much older friends. Some of my same age college friends were deep because we shared our childhood experiences and pain with each other. Many times we find our people out of struggle, hurt, overcoming, and healing.

An unexpected consequence of being young with a disability is that you are always alone in the adult world. From doctor appointments, to lab tests, and x-rays or medical procedures to physical and occupational therapy visits, you are always alone with an adult or in a small group of adults. Likewise, students that need support staff at school also develop trusted adult relationships with their paraprofessional helpers. When a child goes through so much medically and grows up quickly because of their conditions and/or these adult environments, one typically seeks more outside relationships with adults or older peers.

My adopted grandmas in my hometown gave me such rich life lessons. Living in an apartment building that was more accessible than previous living spaces made all the difference in the world. I could visit neighbors in common areas as well as go into all of the apartments. Again, when we live everyday life together and weather the storms life brings, it strengthens our roots and helps us grow deeper. These adopted grandmas were two little cuties who represented my past, as they had stories from different generations of my local family as well as connections to my forefathers in Sweden. One of my adopted grandmothers is a cousin to the couple who watched out for Jaime and I in our townhome. I reconnected with him many times due to this additional "family" tie.

While I was growing up, several of my friends had their great grandparents around for a bit of their childhood, and many of these friends are just now losing their grandparents as we reach middle age. I lost my first grandparent when I was four years old and my last grandparent in my 30s. My adopted grandmas filled a void for me.

I loved having grandmother figures just down the hall in my apartment building. We played many games of Scrabble, Bananagrams, Mexican Train Dominoes, and more. I love playing games and they indulged me by showing interest in learning new games, even if they didn't like the game. They were true grandmas. We cooked together and shared food a lot. We even started a Saturday night dinner group for our whole apartment building. Lots of new friendships and neighborly relationships started, or became deeper, around our potluck style meals and game nights.

One Thanksgiving season I was inspired to make full turkey dinners with all the fixings and dessert for all the residents in our building that would like one. It was quite the undertaking making four turkeys, four pans of mashed potatoes, all the traditional sides, and enough pumpkin bars for over 40 people. It took many ovens, the helping hands of my PCAs, and frequent calls to my mom and sister who are our family's amazing cooks and bakers. I even persuaded a bachelor in the building to use his oven for the first and probably only time as part of this undertaking. We all still talk about this adventure, and not just because I left the gizzard and parts in one of the turkeys. Oops!

One Christmas we had a very powerful snowstorm that trapped us in our building. The winds were so strong and the snow so heavy we were fearful of losing power. So we all started making food and invited the whole building, especially those able to walk our stairs, to come to the alcove on our floor so we could dine together on Christmas. There were around 10 of us and it was a random spread of food, but it was one of my best memories; it was living out the true meaning of Christmas and Christian Fellowship. We never did lose power during our meal, which was a blessing.

Relationships and times of influence happen most in everyday life— our comings and goings. Many times I dismiss the importance of the off chance discussions or greetings of fellow neighbors, and that is not wise. Our simple hellos and asking how you are doing, when you truly mean it and listen, can turn someone's day or even chapter in life to the next new page. My adopted grandmothers were also built-in accountability and pace setters. If my teaching and ministry world got out of balance and I didn't have time for calls or for sharing food, I heard about it. Many times I received gentle reminders to take care of myself and other times, with blunt directness, I heard things like, "You haven't seen me or called me since…" I miss their love, care, and endless pantry provisions when I bake and cook. What I miss the most are the memories we made doing the simplest of tasks. *Life is far better when we have wise friends and strong elders to lead and guide our paths.*

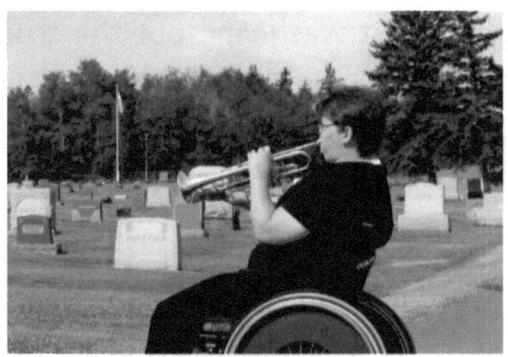

Playing TAPS at a funeral, 2005. Photo taken by Adopted Grandma Marie.

Chapter 12

Bionic Options and a True Friend

"A friend loves at all times, and a brother is born for a time of adversity."
Proverbs 17:17 NIV

As I have shared before, I had been to the Mayo Clinic in Rochester, MN as a child for my diagnosis and beginning stages of treatment. However, early in my teaching career, I returned to see the inventor of finger replacements to consider my options moving forward in life. Over time, my fingers, hands, and wrists became more impacted by JRA with more pain, less function, and decreased strength. I went with my older sister for a quick day trip, and left with new sleeping and resting braces for both arms. I also left armed with information to ponder. Joint replacements for fingers was new technology, and doctors told me I needed to decide if I wanted function or strength in each joint. as you can not have both, yet. Over two decades later I still have non-surgical hands as my legs and elbow needed surgeries. I am sure at some point I will try some finger and wrist surgeries, so I can continue living a life that is as independent and functional as possible. But so far these changing hands can get me through life just fine.

During this time I became a long-term prednisone user. There were many new arthritis medications on the market due to research breakthroughs which was great for others. However, for me, having six total joint replacements created a high risk of infections, so experimenting with these new medications was not wise. I was also tired of feeling like a test dummy or lab rat, so I disappointed my rheumatologist and sided with my orthopedic surgeons, because they had rebuilt this vessel with all of my replacement surgeries. Plus, the thought of having all six joints removed and becoming a puddle of parts in a hospital bed while they cleared out infections was NOT something I was willing to go through. I had seen a friend in a wheelchair go through a hip replacement infection, and he came back to high school sitting in his powerchair without a hip joint. No, Thank You!!! I would not live life without an elbow, hip, two knees, and two ankles! Forget that! So years went by with my medical team fighting each other and me continuing on prednisone. Each time I had my a1c checked, a blood test to show my average blood sugars in the three month period, my internal med doctor would fight with rheumatology about possible diabetes. They didn't like my sugar numbers, but they were using the charts for non-prednisone patients and not the charts that are closest to my conditions. This was a huge difference, since prednisone messes with the sugar content in your blood and how your body processes food and inflammation. Long term prednisone use can greatly impact many of the body's systems. After about five years of this I finally became a real Type 2 diabetic. I chose to go straight to insulin as the other man-made meds make you sick and have bathroom issues. As a wheelchair user making restroom stops can be a considerable time commitment, and very few restrooms meet our accessibility needs. Also, being a music teacher with set lunch and prep times made additional bathroom needs nearly impossible. The medical world needs both better training and experience to fully see the whole patient, rather than focusing on one specialty or medical need in their patient's life.

DJ and I, 2021

Friendships begin at some of the unlikeliest places, and many times out of places of great hurt and need of healing. My most current road trippin' adventure friend, DJ, started as a neighbor, then a friend, then a PCA, and now a dearly trusted friend. We have a great treasure trove of memories on the road from local day trips to road trips to Decorah, trips for fun or checking off some bucket lists, as well as work related and medical trips. DJ could write her own book as she has many amazing stories to tell but, they are hers to tell. I will say that her life intersecting mine when it did has been a saving grace. We just get each other. We can go from acting like silly little school girls, to discussing deep faith-based or life changing topics. We can also be off the wall mad as heck and deeply real about horrendous hurts we are experiencing or remembering. We fiercely have each other's back and can be honest without judgment or backlash. She has been my hands and feet for many years. Now she is experiencing her own medical issues, and is accommodating her everyday spaces and needs based on our shared experiences. When you are someone who needs the help of others daily, there is no greater gift than giving back some help. In this season of our friendship, it has been a healing balm to me when DJ expresses gratitude for seeing my life from my chair and medical needs, because she sees my strength and experiences as something to learn from. Her approach to my life is a welcomed contrast to many other past relationships where I was the one you didn't want to become. I was their motivation to work harder or live life differently, because they didn't want to live a life like mine. Our words have power, so choose them carefully. Our words have power to heal, so share appreciation and gratitude for others, because you don't know what they are facing or how your words might provide healing.

Chapter 13
My Unexpected Pivot

"Leadership. You have to do it yourself, but you can't do it alone." - Blandin Community Leadership Program

In 2016 two of my medical team members surprised me with a nomination for the Miller Dwan Foundation Journey Award. The Journey Award is given to an individual who has made a lasting impact on the disability community as well as advocating for more accessibility. At this point in life I was surgery free for many years and in maintenance mode with my physical goals. I was teaching music full time and really in the prime of life. The nomination and beginning of seeing how others saw me was quite life changing. My two providers who nominated me knew me from my high school and early college days. One was my PT and the other my OT (Occupational Therapist). They had both seen me on my greatest days and in my hardest, tearfilled, painful and frustrating seasons. I was in a long hiatus from my advocacy work, as I was really still healing from all the discrimination and system hurts. I always pushed myself extra hard, partly because I am a Type A and have very high expectations of myself. But honestly, I felt like I had to do more and be more to "make up for what I lack due to my disability." Our inner voices are harsh enough when we enter disability culture, but the daily physical and attitudinal barriers telling you that you are broken and not enough to be a valued or an equal person in the active, non-disabled world are CONSTANT.

Having my providers believe in me and take their precious time to nominate me for the Journey Award, and the humbling honor of receiving the award ignited a fire and strength in me that I had not felt in a very long time. I have always tried to leave spaces and people better than how I found them, as this was ingrained in me from a young age. But this award ceremony was a culmination of all my worlds coming together— my family, my church family, my medical family, my work world, as well as leaders and role models who were part of my journey since childhood. This spark gave birth to a fire and awareness in me: I do not want the current and future families impacted by childhood disability to go through the heartaches and challenges my family and I went through in our small town and region. There is a gut level passion of activism that fuels the changes inside of me, and these feelings surprised me.

Small, rural towns have difficulty finding the funding and resources to support their basic needs and utilities. Raising accessibility funding for what seems like just a few people in your town can be nearly impossible. With more education, experiences, and lobbying this trend is slowly changing as the disabled community is the largest minority world wide. The most frustrating aspect of the ADA is that it is the largest unfunded law in the US which impacts every area of life.

For this awards ceremony I was able to invite family, friends, and colleagues. It was staggering to see so many people from my journey in one space. Even my first grade teacher surprised me and attended! She was one of my biggest supporters in my elementary days, even though she was my teacher before I got sick.

As I delivered my speech and connected with each of my invitees with eye contact and smiles, it was all so surreal. I love when my worlds collide and important people in each area of life get to meet each other. Each relationship has its purpose and course, some are destined for the long haul while others have changes and even endings.

This awards banquet also marked the clear ending to a toxic relationship that had been a nurturing one long ago. In my grief over the relationship, I had forgotten the goodness of God and how, when He is removing one thing, He already has even better things in store.

The following year someone told me about the Blandin Community Leadership Program (BCLP) cohort opportunity. BCLP required a week away at a retreat center in the middle of our state, as well as several full day meetings as retreat follow-up trainings. This program was designed to cover costs of lost work time, so my eight days of substitute teachers were covered at no cost to me, I just had to create the hours of sub lesson plans. I had a few friends that went through this program years earlier, and even though I was a complete newbie, I decided to go to the informational meeting. My lack of self confidence preceded me, and I felt very unworthy of sharing a space with some of these already amazing leaders. I was concerned about accessibility of the building and property where I would be staying, and also the attitudes and personalities of the trainers and my cohort peers. So I prayed about this exciting and yet terrifying opportunity.

Whew! I was chosen as an alternate which, to me, was perfect. I was wanted, but I didn't have to commit to going or to the challenge. Well, that was short lived as our cohort grew by two spots and then I was going! Normally in life I need a Personal Care Attendant (PCA) to help with daily living needs in the mornings. But in my gut I just knew if I brought along one of my PCAs I would constantly be concerned about them, their needs, and their comfort levels. I would be greatly distracted from my need to be changed, to be inspired, and to be filled by positive intentions for growth and change. How would I be able to go, have my basic needs met, and still be just me?

One of the fellow cohort members was a long time leader and nurse. She is someone I had unconsciously looked up to since middle school when we girls start looking at female roles and leaders. So I summoned my courage to ask a stranger for help with my morning care needs. and she answered with a resounding yes! We had an interesting week of learning about resort bathrooms that are semi accessible, and how shoes need to be far away from the shower!

Going solo to the resort center was SUCH a huge adventure for me. I traveled alone through the very rural and remote areas of our state where there are no gas stations or towns for very long stretches, and definitely no accessible gas stations or bathrooms for the whole trip! Upon my arrival, a very friendly front desk worker was completely willing to come to my vehicle and carry all my luggage and accessibility tools in for me. When I travel I literally have to bring everything AND the kitchen sink as so much of my daily life is tailored to me in my daily surroundings. When you go to new spaces you have no idea how you will have to change and adjust to that environment, so you bring above and beyond what you need at home.

The staff at the resort truly were authentic in their inclusivity and servant heart. At every meal I felt like a famous person being asked if I needed help or wanted certain things. They were very accommodating, and not overbearing or intrusive at all. It felt SO foreign, and just beyond nice - how life can and should be for everyone.

Our leadership training times were indescribable experiences of great growth, introspection, self reflection, and team building. Many of the cohort names, faces, and leadership roles they held were familiar to me, but many of us were complete strangers when we started. Our retreat of four full days felt like weeks long when we look back at that time of growth. By the third day, we were a happy little family whom the leaders struggled to quiet so we could get to their presentations and our work.

Our cohort was very encouraging, and after the first night with the campfire located in a less than optimal accessible location, my fellow Blandees worked with resort staff to move it so the experience could be enjoyed by all. This simple gesture by my new friends made my eyes and heart swell with tears, because it is so rare in life to find non-disabled people willing to change sometimes very simple things to be more inclusive. By this small act of a few, all were able to play games, sing songs, laugh, and dream big. This night together led to the work I do today and its mission— "to make the North Shore a destination for people with disabilities." One of my Blandin brothers was paying attention and gracefully coined this phrase.

The leadership skills, relationships, partnerships, and humanity that the

retreat and leadership program guides much of my advocacy work today. The memories of how accepted my nurse friend, the resort workers, my new Blandin family and the trainers made me feel, and just the heart in that space, ignites my spirit still today. The way many of our cohort members returned home and began embracing inclusion in all of the festivals and events our town puts on was outstanding! Their work continues today, not just within our small town, but in all the new locations our Blandin family finds themselves living in as they work near and far.

When the quiet, introverted side of me looks at this huge adventure I embarked on alone, relying on strangers, being more vulnerable and real than I had been in a very long time, or really ever in this large of a setting, I am shocked. And in this shock I see the provision of my Savior going before me, alongside me, and as my rearguard. He provided my every need and beyond. He created relationships that went beyond me ast the one in need. I experienced deep conversations and bonds with people I would have never known in the general sense, let alone at these deep, vulnerable, leader levels. We all have needs if we are truly honest with ourselves. Some needs are just more visible than others, but we all have them, every day.

Seeing the freshness and excitement in others around advocacy and inclusion in our community relit my burned-out advocate wick. I came home looking at life and obstacles in ways I used to see them and talk about them. It was as if the scales of oppression had fallen from my eyes and I saw the world as it should be; not as me being "a less than" groveling to be invited to the front sidewalk of the inaccessible party.

There was a new confidence and strength within me. I had continually shared my experiences, new knowledge and skills with my dear friends, which also helped me solidify and be accountable to these life changes. At some of our final celebrations I found myself boldly challenging certain community leaders, who once intimidated me, to make their organizations more inclusive. Our students and families deserve better from us, and they should not experience what my parents had to go through with me. It felt like an out of body experience as my heart, hurt, and truth came out of my mouth. The impact on these people and their leadership roles is still developing today. This was another God moment with me as a willing mouthpiece and an example of how lives are interconnected, creating a tapestry of relationships.

If my medical providers hadn't nominated me for the Journey Award, I would have never considered applying for the Blandin Community Leadership Program, or developed the passion and skills to share my story and impact local leaders.

Chapter 14

Strong Sisters

"Though one may be overpowered, two can defend themselves. A cord of three strands is not quickly broken." Ecclesiastes 4:12 NIV

When I was in my late twenties, I began to self reflect on my life thus far. During this time I had a childhood mentor who very quickly passed away from cancer. These were hard times to say the least, as this friend was the first person to give me a Bible that wasn't a church issued version. She was one of my first friends that shared real, everyday life with me. She was ever the encourager and educator. She always had laughs and kind words for others, even when her world was shaken or hurting.

It was during this journey that I researched my medical records to find my date of diagnosis, both locally and at the Mayo Clinic. Of the two dates, I chose the local date of February 25, 1988, to be the anniversary I would celebrate. Just as cancer survivors have a date that defines a life changing moment, I now use my diagnosis anniversary to remember how far I have come, what I have lived through, and what I am thankful and grateful for in spite of what this date means to my journey. Ultimately, this date is like a remembrance stone in my faith walk, to remind me of the Lord's faithfulness as I have crawled, walked, and wheeled through this life.

You see, this generic date has been used by myself and my family for decades. This huge life change was the pivot point on the family calendar that my family referenced almost daily. "That happened before Jenna got sick." "I believe that happened a few months after Jenna got sick." I thought, if this date has such power and influence in our lives, then by all means let's celebrate and name this pivotal date.

In 2018 I celebrated the 30th anniversary of my diagnosis. Many people I shared my celebration plans with thought I was weird, especially my family. But I knew they needed time to come to terms with it on their own, and I was used to being the odd or different duck in my family. The celebration was not just about me or for me; it was also about the people who walked alongside me and carried me through these 30 years. I began my preparations by praying for direction and confirmation of this weird, new event. I started writing very heartfelt letters of gratitude to my family, friends, and long-term medical providers. The process was long and emotionally hard, but it was through this letter writing journey that I so richly saw the tapestry of love, care, and friendship that was woven together by the hands of God. I used at least a box of Kleenex as I wrote these many letters. During this time, I was also working at walking and climbing stairs for my health and for future opportunities, and my letter writing inspired me to have standing photos taken with these strong pillars of relationships in my life.

I need to make a side note here to explain why a standing picture was part of this inspiration for me. As a wheelie who is proud of her journey, the good, the bad and the ugly, I am a whole person who lives in both disabled and non-disabled cultures. For me, the people who received letters from me love me unconditionally, and it doesn't matter if I am wheeling or walking in their lives, they support all of me. These pictures of me standing eye to eye, and many times with my eyes above theirs for the first time, are symbolic of the strength and confidence they have given me in my life. For me, standing was expressing that strength and gratitude in new found ways, and for me standing and walking is a gauge to the health of my joint replacements and medical health, which is only possible in spurts. During this time of my life I was working hard at fighting through old behaviors, hurts, and unhealthy relationships that I was finally strong enough to leave. So, there is a lot of personal symbolism in these standing photos, and not about conforming to ableist viewpoints.

An ableist viewpoint of these pictures would be one of pity or of unwarranted inspiration. Many times people with disabilities or medical issues are turned into other people's muse or source of inspiration. In reality, we are just living the life we have been given. I am proud of my disability and who I am with it and in spite of it. These standing pictures represent me taking control of my life and honoring those people who have stood by me in the good times and, more importantly, the hard times. Standing is symbolic for me as I have endured and healed through 12 orthopedic surgeries, which includes six total joint replacements. Being vertical is a health promoting position for me as I need my osteoporotic bones to grow, and my internal organs to have space to function. Both of these medical needs can be most easily addressed through weight bearing and standing. I no longer wish for a cure of my disease, but for kindness, inclusion, authentic curiosity from others, and spaces that are safe and inclusive for all people. I am blessed by my large support system, and each picture represents more than a thousand stories that make us who we are.

Besides these letters and photos, I wanted to bless some of the strongest

Christian women who have fought beside me in many different realms of my life. My dear friend and PCA, DJ, helped me plan a night of thanks on

I worked with a local coffee shop owner, who was also a Blandin alum from a different cohort, to rent her space as it was truly Jenna-friendly, including the restrooms! DJ and I planned the menu of many favorite recipes, as I enjoy expressing my love and care through cooking and baking. We also looked through all my photos, from childhood to current, for table decor. I printed all the standing pictures and framed them to be the place cards marking where my dearly loved guests of honor would sit for our dinner and presentation together. I was also able to use Skype so Jaime, Lisa and Lisa's oldest daughter, Bretta, could participate in this special time together, and meet some of the other Strong Women of Faith who nurtured me into the woman I was beginning to fully grasp and appreciate.

The week before my anniversary, I was out of town at the music educators state convention where I saw my dear friend and mentor, Fitz. We had a nice lunch together. I shared my letter with her and we took an updated standing picture together. I also saw my college trumpet buddy,

Brian. We enjoyed a great dinner out in the big city as well as a standing picture.

This is the same Brian/trumpet buddy whose wife, Morgan, would get bored with his constant talk of music gear and technology. When this happened, she threw me under the bus and asked him if he talked to me lately. Instead, Brian would call me and talk for hours while Morgan got a break from her hubby. Full circle from being threatened by me to using me as a means to some quiet time. Haha

In true Jenna fashion, the Lego robotics team I coached for many hours weekly for over six years, advanced to their first ever State Championship. Yes, it was scheduled for the day before my celebration event. DJ was a champ, and we dug deep to prepare all the party needs before heading to State together. Looking back, it was a whirlwind and I am unsure how we got it all done, but these memories and the bonding that happened between DJ and I during this time built a strong foundation for all the things we would weather together in the future. How good is our God!

The frenzied day of traveling home from State, working on preparations while on the road, and finishing the final touches for the event all came to a grinding halt when my dear friends began to arrive. The peace that passes all understanding took over, and all the details and final touches faded away because "my tribe" had arrived. I wanted to make sure each honored guest felt safe and seen. I know many of these dear friends are similar to me in the social awkwardness of meeting new people. In kindness, I made sure they each had a familiar person seated near them and then a new friend I really wanted them to meet.

I wanted to create a warm and cozy physical space conveying the thankfulness and appreciation my heart and spirit felt for these special women. Some of these ladies had been a part of my life for decades, and some for just a year or so. It doesn't matter the quantity of time we spend, but the quality of time we spend together which makes footprints on our lives and hearts. My heart bursts when I think of this special night. The fear of the vulnerability I was facing was extreme, but I just knew this was where I needed to be, expressing and returning blessings to women who had richly blessed me. I knew this was my next step in my leadership journey.

The setting sun glowed through the restaurant's large windows creating an atmosphere of closeness and intimacy. It was time for me to read their letters. To sit in front of these women and bare my life story in little vignettes was scary and thrilling at the same time. I was concerned how they would feel having some of their stories shared through me in front of the room of friends, acquaintances, and strangers, so I made sure the stories were focused on my journey and their help along the way. Each letter was full of smiles, laughter, and tears as each tender time was completed by long heart to heart hugs. Sharing gratitude and one's heart can be risky and anxiety producing but, it can also be restorative and healing.

Chapter 15

Hotel Soup

"Only the pure in heart can make a good soup."
- Beethoven

Traveling with a wheelchair can be a challenge to say the least. There is a LOT of prep work in finding the right hotels, following up with a hotel to make sure your reservation is correct, then dealing with all the changes once you arrive. On our first trip to Mayo, DJ and I stayed at a hotel chain that is known for better accessibility. When I travel, I look for pool lifts to access the hot tub and pool. Since I do the majority of the driving, I need a warm space with jets to loosen up the tension I build up while driving five to six hours in a day. We also chose this hotel over others as they offered a wheelchair accessible shuttle, which is a very rare find in Minnesota.

Upon arrival, we were greeted by the smell of soup and food. This was my first experience visiting a hotel that offered complimentary breakfast as well as complementary soup dinners. After long days of being poked and prodded in the medical setting, this warm light meal was a welcomed experience. We hopped into the hot tub only to find a frayed mechanical cord that worked intermittently. We discovered this issue after I was already down in the hot tub and prayed our way out of it. The next day, maintenance wrapped the wires in tape to provide a safer experience.

The following morning we had our first shuttle experience. It was a typical hotel shuttle with a wheelchair lift in the back portion. When we went outside, the lift was waiting for me. I wheeled on just like the millions of times I rode in our school bus. Once inside, the experience was VERY different. Instead of facing forward, I faced sideways. DJ is an experienced school bus driver from her previous career and knew how to tie me down and... oh wait, there were no tie downs. Oh, and the driver could not get the ramp to fold back up so they could close the door. The hotel staff had to grab the maintenance man, who was a spitting image of my funny, quick witted cousin. While he helped the driver get the ramp back in the shuttle (thanks to DJ and I knowing about the hydraulic manual option), the maintenance man hopped on the shuttle to help us when we arrived at Mayo. Well, I was in my manual wheelchair with no seat belt or tie downs. DJ was positioned in a seat next to me holding on to my wheelchair. The maintenance man was in the jump seat in the back right next to me holding on to my chair for dear life, and I was holding on to him and the seat in front of me. Halfway to our destination, the maintenance man finally put his seatbelt on after we had a very hard left turn, and he realized we needed at least one of us strapped in. This was quite the illegal adventure, BUT we lived to tell the tale! We also never rode the shuttle again. The hotel staff apologized profusely, and kept saying they just had it in for inspection and fixing— *this is usually the pat answer/comment when things don't go as planned with accessibility technology.*

During these interesting times with the main-tenance man, we built a rapport. He even made us his famous chicken wild rice soup and left it in our room fridge while we were gone to the doctors one day. I know this sounds weird and unsafe as I write this, but in the moment it was just a really kind and thoughtful gesture from a thoughtful young man who cared about his job and the people he influences.

The Mayo Clinic is a HUGE and confusing campus at first sight. There is marble everywhere and tons of people, depending on which building you are in. I was beyond thankful for DJ and her expertise in knowing where to go, hidden ways of getting through human traffic, and the best places and times of day to eat. It was weird being the new kid on the block at a medical facility. At my local clinic, I can say hi to many people using first names, but here they were all strangers. No shared memories. No staff that knew my story and the hurts behind my smiles and jokes. Just the business at hand.

The first doctor I saw was an internal medicine doctor who asked me to call her Tej. She was very kind. These offices were so weird. First we entered a VERY quiet office-like room. When it was time for the medical exam, a side door opened leading to a typical looking exam room. However, this room was too small for a wheelchair user, and the exam table height didn't adjust to allow for a transfer. We went down the hall to a procedure room that met my needs. During our time together, Tej watched me have a diabetic episode when I was unable to talk and could only cry. She immediately gave me some candy and a nurse ran to get orange juice. She determined that my current local doctors were controlling my diabetes too tightly which caused lows, and I did not know what was happening to me. From that day on I took only oral diabetic meds and not insulin. She also made a plan for all my future appointments during my week at Mayo. I saw a rheumatologist and two endocrinologists—one for my osteoporosis and one for my diabetes and long term prednisone use.

After all my x-rays, the first doctor I met was a veteran female surgeon who went to medical school with my new-to-me local surgeon. Her hands noticeably shook. When she left the room, I told DJ there was no way this lady would be doing my surgery. When the doctor returned, she eased my fears by saying she no longer did surgery, but does intakes and decides who is emergent and needs surgery sooner than later. That eased my fears but also annoyed me, as I knew I probably needed surgery, so this appointment was a waste of my time until I could see my actual surgeon. Unfortunately, I was unable to see my "real surgeon" during this several day stay at Mayo.

I saw the rheumatologist, but unlike my childhood memory, this doctor had no oak shelves or leather chairs, just the typical clinical space. He was very knowledgeable and taught me the new name for my disease— Juvenile Idiopathic Arthritis. This new title made SO much sense, as I never fit the rheumatoid arthritis model as a child, or actually ever. I always tease my doctors that if their little doctor book says do ABC to fix me, they need to do QRS. And many times this has rung true. I was disappointed only in the fact that this doctor had never seen someone like me with six joint replacements. The greatest number he had seen in a patient was four. I was and am still tired of being a medical phenomenon when it comes to joint replacements, as I have met others with even more replacements than me. I never seem to find the right docs that don't see me as the exception. He was also very knowledgeable about one of my medications, methotrexate, and had practiced medicine and research all over Australia and Europe. He validated my local medical team's avoidance of rDNA medications, due to the possibility of joint infections and the serious complications that would cause.

My two endocrinologists were interesting. One was older, probably near retirement, and reminded me of the newscaster, Walter Cronkite. He was kind, but talked way above my head. (DJ fell fast asleep in this appointment which kept me awake and entertained). We made a plan to wean me off prednisone, which included follow ups and tests with my local doctors to monitor my internal organs and glands, and avoid an endocrine crash or thyroid issues. My second doctor was a bit older than me and wore a plastic pocket protector— I kid you not— I could not stop looking at it! Though he was very knowledgeable about medications for osteoporosis, I taught him more about side effect issues as a wheelchair user. For decades, and still today, I need to remind doctors about the whole person they are treating. While a bathroom issue might seem like a nuisance to an ambulatory person or person with good hands, it can disable and stop the productive life of a chair user. The time it takes for me to use the restroom is 5—10 times longer than my non-disabled friends and family. Also, some side effects that can just be an annoyance when sitting or in certain positions can be a no go for someone who has to sit all day. In this session I feel like we made good plans for my osteoporosis and future surgery needs, but was disappointed and frustrated when I returned home to my doctor. The notes that the Mayo doctor wrote to him were completely backwards from what we discussed in person. I am ever thankful for my great memory and attention to detail, but some days I just long for systems to work and function in the ways they were truly designed to . I am concerned for the day that I don't have my wits about me and can't help my medical team do and plan what is best for me.

Reflection:

One of the attributes that is core to my personhood is making time for people and relationships. This is no different when I am traveling.

I have been blessed so many times by taking an extra hour and spending a longer lunch with extended family of my own, or of my traveling companions. I vividly remember my first extended family visit with a former friend and her aunt and uncle when we were out exploring. She was very grateful for the time with her family, and it was an unexpected blessing as it was one of the last times she saw her uncle. I have had similar times with my family, especially on my medical trips to Mayo, seeing family on the way down or while I was there. I reconnected with my aunts and uncles who relocated closer to Mayo for their medical needs, as well as my college friends and their new families. On one of my Mayo trips, my dear friend DJ and I braved a blizzard-like November snow storm to meet my extended family for dinner at a local BBQ place. I got to meet my "cool cousin" and his wife and son. It was a night of laughter, sharing life and trying new foods like fried okra. Only a few months later their jubilant, young, foodie son went to heaven. Even though we only met Austin once, his life and love of life made a profound impact on DJ and me.

If I can impart any wisdom to you, my beloved reader, seize today to create space for relationships. Leave margins in your travel plans so you can make lasting and impactful memories, because our time here is precious, FULL of purpose, and fleeting

Chapter 16

Step Up to the Toilet

"Hope everything comes out ok!" - Unknown

A few months later I traveled to Mayo Clinic again, but this time with my oldest sister. I saw two orthopedic surgeons on this day. The first one was for my ankle that has a crunchy replacement in it. My ankles were done back in early college days and well past their function dates, but since I wasn't up and walking everyday they were able to last me longer. This surgeon was a very young guy but he welcomed my hard questions about the lack of good, strong bone in my legs, ankles and feet, the possible use of a bone growth stimulator, and the possibility of amputation if surgeries don't go smoothly. He was the first surgeon

I heard say the word amputation. While others shy away from hard conversations, I am the type of person who needs information and ideas for different options. For me, fear of the unknown is FAR greater than discussing and planning for worst case scenarios that rarely happen. I wasn't sure that this specific surgeon was right for me, but I really did appreciate his bedside manner and truthfulness in answering my hard questions.

Then it was time for my knee surgeon, but before I could see him I needed more x-rays to be seen by the surgeon's student. By this time my knee felt a bit more stable, but not quite right as there were some clunks from time to time. During the student's examination, he had me lay on my back as he manipulated my knee in different ways of flexion and extension. To me it didn't feel that bad, just a little extra wiggle. After he left, the surgeon, Dr. Taunton, came in. He sat me up on the side of the exam table with my leg dangling during the whole exam. In this position I felt a TON of joint loosening and instability. He asked to be excused to get his student. I could tell by his tone, mannerisms, and my previous surgical experiences that this was not good. After he left, I teared up, looked at my sister and told her I needed surgery. She was shocked I could get all of this from the 30 second exam. Sure enough, he brought in his student and asked him many questions about my first exam and how he performed it. I could tell by his body tension and voice that he was not happy, but the teacher in me knew this was a valuable teachable moment. I was right, I needed surgery, and sooner than later. I wanted to push it out until the following summer due to my teaching calendar, but that was not possible. The earliest date available was September 11, 2019. I agreed to this date— my teacher bestie's wedding anniversary, Lisa's daughter's birthday, and the anniversary of the most tragic event in American history I had lived through. But I knew in my gut and my spirit that this doctor was trustworthy and at the top of his game. I have to admit that I was mad though, as my local doctors all assessed me in the same position as the student, on my back, and thus never fully saw the limitation and instability I was complaining and concerned about. Many months of uncertainty, pain, and nervousness could have been avoided had the local surgeons examined me in the correct position. BUT, everything has a reason and a season.

Before my first surgery at Mayo, my father had some medical issues of his own. Traveling to Rochester for my surgery, staying in hotels and sitting all day wouldn't work for him. I know he felt bad and probably guilty, as he had been at all of my previous surgeries. So DJ, my mom, and my two sisters made the trek. DJ and I left a few days ahead as I had some pre-surgery appointments and scans.

DJ was a gem and called around to make the hotel reservations. We had asked for a wheelchair accessible room with a roll-in shower in a hotel with a pool lift—my usual accommodation needs. As we drove around the block at this hotel, I had a bad feeling. It looked old— Pre ADA— before 1990. It had high sidewalks all around the front with one accessible but steep curb cut by the restaurant, rather than by the hotel's front door. The doors were not button powered or automatic. As they say, "Don't judge a book by its cover." We proceeded. The front desk was very friendly, timely, and helpful. We went up the elevator to our room. The room was very small and narrow. As we went through the entry hall of the room, we could see a loveseat in front of the TV. Confusing. Around the corner we saw a full size, not queen size, bed against the wall with the loveseat at the foot of the bed. This was not a pullout couch as promised, and I don't believe there was room to get a wheelchair on either side of the bed. I was SO claustrophobic. The bathroom near the room's entrance was another long and narrow space with a roll-in shower straight across from the entry door. However, the bath bench attached to the wall was mounted only a foot from the floor. There would be no transferring to something that low. We were so flabbergasted by the shower that we totally missed the toilet.. As we backed up, because there was no room to turn my chair around, we spotted the toilet to our left. It was literally wedged between two walls as if it was installed in a closet. And then we looked down... the toilet was installed on top of a stair. One would literally have to step up and turn around to use the toilet. This was not wheelchair friendly in any sense. DJ and I were completely speechless as we had NEVER seen anything like this. I keep kicking myself for not taking any pictures of this mind-blowing room, because no one can believe the inaccessibility of this space. *In the back of my mind I kind of wondered if I was secretly being pranked.*

We made our way down to the front desk where the nice assistant was overwhelmed by people checking in. I explained my accessibility needs and how the current room was not ADA compliant. I asked if there were any better accessible rooms available. . She said no, they are all the same and all checked out. So I asked about their public bathrooms, as I have rented inaccessible rooms in the past but was able to use a public or pool bathroom that was up to code. DJ and I looked at all options and all toilets were great— for toddlers, not adults, and definitely not wheelchair accessible. We asked for her help in finding accessible accommodations since they clearly are non-compliant. She truly wasn't much help, so DJ and I started calling around. This is not the experience you want after driving for five hours, a few days before surgery, at a major medical institution that is new to you and your family. We finally settled on the Country Inn where my sister and I stayed months earlier, and they were absolutely amazing!

Spaces and places may be in compliance with the ADA by checking off the boxes of code standards. Committed spaces and staff see and care about the whole person and their experience beyond the physical infrastructure and code. Commitment over compliance is the goal.

The night before surgery, I talked to my local pediatric orthopedic surgeon. We have some family connections. It was great getting his call on my cell to ease my concerns over this first surgery without him and my local team. Dr. Taunton, the Mayo surgeon, wanted me to have a spinal block. I had never had one before, and with my spine curvatures and osteoporosis, I was scared. But my local surgeon reminded me that I was now a little fish in the big pond, that my medical complications were nothing for them at Mayo, and that they deal with way more complicated cases than mine each day. So I trusted my doctor's advice to trust these new doctors.

The day of surgery arrives. I had to arrive extra early, as they did not get a needed x-ray the day before. DJ dropped me off for the scheduled x-ray while my family arrived in another area. I do not remember much about the morning except that I had to urinate all the time. You have to love nerves and also our humanness; often when you're told you can't do something, that is all you want to do. A very nice nurse came into the staging area and gave us privacy briefs my new surgeon had designed. This was something new to me, but it made total sense to avoid the birthday suit scenario since they were just working on my knee. My mom was a trouper and tried to help me get these things on. They literally came up to my knees. I knew I gained a little extra weight from the inactivity with my knee, but SERIOUSLY? It was humiliating and funny at the same time. DJ and my sisters came in and tried to offer help or ideas. A bit later the nurse came back, and I made a joke about the privacy briefs and she got red faced...she had given me a pediatric pair! No wonder I could not get them above the knee! Well, the adult ones worked just fine and are highly recommended. We all laughed and laughed.

My mom came to the pre-op room with me, even when I was an adult. I have many orthopedic and mobility issues to consider, and usually I do just fine as a self advocate, but depending on when they make you sleepy that can be a challenge for me. At Mayo, they have policies against family coming with you. My oldest sister, who is the most protective, and I pushed the issue, so she could accompany me once she did some paperwork. After I had a tear filled "see ya later" with DJ, my mom, and my other sister, we were rushed off to the pre-op area. The pre-op space was SO tiny and had glass walls almost like an ICU room. There was more poking, prodding and exams than I had for all of my previous surgeries combined. We repeatedly had to remind them of my other joint replacements and my fused right elbow. The time came to say goodbye to my sister and it all got very, very real. From here on it was me, God, Jesus, the Holy Spirit and my new medical team. I entered the cold, sterile and very busy operating room. I met my anesthetist, a handsome Black man with a British accent. He was a welcomed distraction from the freezing cold nervousness ahead, but I sensed he was slowly making me sleepy as I strained to understand his questions through his accent. Then the anesthesiologist came in to give me my spinal block. I had my script from my local doctor about my scoliosis and the locations of my curves memorized. He took a minute to recheck my back scans before touching my back. When he returned he said, "Oh I've got you. Your curves are nothing compared to what I see everyday." The next thing I know, he is asking if my left leg is numb. I took a few seconds to consult my body. This concerned him. I said, "Nope, my left leg can feel everything but my right leg is as dead as a doornail." He tried to cover his concern but said, "Interesting. How about now?" I consulted my body and then said, "Yes, the left one is slowly fading but the right is still dead." And within moments I was down for the count.

The next thing I knew, some female voice was yelling and telling me I was done and to wake up so they could bring me to post-op. It felt like waking up from a nap. By the time I was wheeled to the recovery room, I knew my nurse's name and the name of the patient next to me. I could relate to her horrible experience of waking up, as it sounded like my previous experiences. I felt very bad for her. In no time at all I was having full conversations with my nurse. When they brought me up to my room, I was sitting up on the gurney and making the nurse laugh. My family knew I was coming before they saw me because they heard my notorious laugh. I heard them talking about me, and their faces showed disbelief at my ability to laugh and carry a full conversation. This was the weirdest experience for me, as usually I am incoherent, crabby and need pain meds after surgery.

The next few post op days and nights were pretty typical. My surgical leg was completely soft casted and unseen until my day of release. During my first night, two male nurses boosted me up in bed, they didn't notice the compression socks hose was wrapped around the end of the bed. When they gave me a yank, I went up but my surgical leg stayed down there. That was NOT fun. They did so much work on my soft tissues that my hip was not happy and needed to be in a bent position, which gave a little flexion to the knee. They did not like this but I did not care. *And I was right, as still today this knee goes completely straight and even hyper extends if I am not careful.*

During my stay in Rochester, I had lots of unexpected visitors from my Cool Cousin Pat and his Cool Wife Robyn, as well as my Iowa Family! I also got snuggles from Yodel, my new surgery stuffed animal. He is a large St. Bernard that looks exactly like my friend's dog, Alice. She was my farm hand at their farm where I have raised garden beds. I usually had Yodel perched on my surgical leg to guard off the pesky nurses and pain causing PTs.

After a few days I was discharged and needed medical transport from Rochester to Duluth. This was new for me as I had always traveled sitting in my chair. Again, DJ the lifesaver, rode home with me to provide company and comfort. Our driver was very nice. My sisters and mom caravaned to get my van and gear back home. Everything was great until we got to the rehab in Duluth where the driver almost decapitated me; he forgot to lower the gurney before pulling me out. Good thing the pain meds had worn off so I could yell to avoid further damage..

As I shared before, nothing goes easy or as needed. The rehab facility was not my first choice and one I had never been to before. When we arrived there were hours and hours of issues with my pain meds. My protective sisters and DJ went round and round with the charge nurse until I finally got my pain meds over 8 hours late! Thank goodness I have a high pain tolerance and family and friends that will advocate until we get what I need.

I wish I could say that my stay at rehab was fabulous and easy, but it was not. Knee replacement surgeries are always a bear to heal from. Many of my nurses were kind and great, but some were very bad. At one point I called out a nurse because she wanted to help me dress my legs in a way that would hurt me. I got owly and said, "If you don't let me do this myself I will not get better, and I will not leave here. I have been through this surgery and rehabs MANY times. Please leave me alone so I can do this safely on my own in ways that work for me." I also added that I am a teacher, and I know the only way to retrain my brain is to let it fail in safe ways, so I can relearn how to do things for myself. She looked at me all confused. She assumed I had MS or some kind of condition. I quickly excused her and told her to go read my chart. DJ picked up a LOT of the nursing slack, because they simply were short staffed and ill equipped.

During my 10 day rehab stay, I made great gains thanks to my short and feisty PT. God always knows which PTs to put in my path. My weekend PTs were lame. I told them what I needed and asked them to increase my reps and expectations. I wanted to avoid problems with my main PT on Monday over lack of work on the weekend. I think that story made my main PT glad that I was self advocating, knew what I had to do, and what was at stake for me. I also think it made her mad that a patient needed to take charge and rule the roost to keep the rehab healing train going.

I had many friends and family visits throughout my stay. That helped the time go by and truly helped the healing process. I am a game playing fool, so when my gaming friends came one evening, I sat in my chair longer than I had since before surgery. We had amazing Chinese food that they smuggled in, too. It was a needed break for DJ and I, even if I paid for it in swelling and pain later that night and the next day. My teacher bestie also came to visit. I can still picture her little face in my barely opened door. I also remember talking a mile a minute so she wouldn't leave anytime soon. When you are used to living life with someone and teaching together twice a week, and you haven't seen each other in over two weeks, you just have to have a motor mouth. No doubt the pain meds also had something to do with it. She just giggles when she thinks about this memory, and how I just kept talking and talking and talking.

Reflection:

> *The history of my medical journey is dotted with times of great isolation, mostly during hospital stays for surgeries, surgical rehabilitations, and changes to medications. Most of these times were faith deepening experiences for me, my family, and my friends. It was always great to see familiar and encouraging faces during these difficult times. I often made acquaintances with fellow patients, and usually I was many decades their junior. My family has always been a rock for me, visiting daily during medical stays, while my adopted family and close friends visited when they could.*

The long nights after visiting hours were the toughest times. Many people think this is when you sleep, rest, and heal, but often it is a battle, the darkest night of the soul. The busyness of the day and constant questions like, "What's your pain level?" "How are you feeling?" "Ready for the next level of activity?" keep your brain active and alert to the requests of others. However, when the hall lights dim and everyone is in their rooms, the doors close, and you are alone with your thoughts and your tiny TV screen. During these times, after a physically and emotionally exhausting day, you know sleep will come eventually. You'll wake to the faces of helpful staff, hopefully to visitors, and to the same cycle being repeated over and over again.

After years of these experiences, both good and hard, I accumulated many tips and tricks to help myself get through these nights. The new technology of cell phones, WiFi, and laptops really broke down some of those nightly closed doors, so I could stay connected to my loved ones, my community, and the world around me. Who knew that these tech skills would become a necessity in the years ahead? Well, of course... God knew.

Chapter 17

Ableism and Isolation

"Think bigger. Think Differently." - Bush
Foundation Fellowship

After many months of being home from Blandin, I received an email from a local foundation saying they selected me to attend a community leadership conference in our state capitol. Again, this was exciting, scary, and intimidating. Remember traveling with the kitchen sink? Off to new surroundings, new relationships, new hotels and locations that could or could not be Jenna-friendly. Thankfully I had DJ, my best traveling adventure friend and PCA, with me because it was an access rollercoaster. After weeks of helping foundation staff with all the right questions to get the best answers from hotel staff, we arrived at the hotel.

This was one of the most confusing hotel accessibility experiences ever, and I have had a lot of them. In hotels we wheelies usually have issues with the beds. Such as, beds that are too high to transfer from wheelchair to bed. For those that need under bed space for a hoyer lift transfer, box frames to the floor are a barrier. For the first and only time at hotels so far, the beds were way too low! After an hour of explaining and educating the front desk and maintenance staff we worked it out, but had to pay for an additional attached room. Our work around was I would sleep in the inaccessible room with the higher bed, and use the restroom in the accessible room while my friend did the reverse. I remember feeling guilty about the foundation paying for an additional inaccessible hotel room to make things accessible for me. It was frustrating, confusing, and exhausting, but I put on my happy face and engaged in an amazing leadership conference.

It was a great conference and I took home many new skills, understandings and connections. I also gained deeper awareness regarding the unknowns of travel, conference planning, and how lack of access can make or break an experience for me.

Since a very young age, I have understood that this world is not friendly to people like me, and it expects us to adapt and change to the man-made systems that created it. Many times there are great, well intentioned people who want to change and be inclusive, but you don't know what you don't know. Then we need to be the teachers and changers. This, on top of being exhausted people who do four times the work preparing for a trip, then four times the work again on arrival. Isn't it just easier and safer to stay home? Sure, but then you miss out on an adventure, on building relationships, and exploring the world around you.

Since my youth, I have struggled with being a burden or the reason loved ones and others needed to do and spend more. I am blessed with many friends and adopted family who have helped me feel differently, as a valued part of their world. These are rare gems of people who can enter into my laugh it off mentality. Oh, don't get me wrong, they can be some of the most protective and frustrated people when I am wronged or hurt by a situation, lack of access, or the rude treatment by others; but after a good vent, we laugh. Sometimes we laugh until we cry.

After getting home from the conference, my mind was swimming with ideas including possible solutions to the systemic accessibility issues in the hospitality industry, and just life in general. The issues were glaring and confusing, and yet to me, so easy to solve. Or so it seemed.

I remember the day sitting in my music classroom, trying to psych myself up to call the president of a local foundation to request connections to some local leaders. Before any big call or meeting, I need quiet time to prepare my brain and mouth for all the possibilities, and things I may need to say. Many times I use more energy and time in the preparations than in the actual call. After all these decades of asking for help, you would think I would be a pro at this...I am not.

Someone had mentioned the Bush Fellowship program to me during my conference, and this intrigued me. A fellowship to get paid to develop myself and my leadership skills, while working on my passion projects of accessibility and advocacy. Yes please! The local foundation president connected me with two Bush Fellows who lived and advocated in our region. These two women became two of the greatest champions of my work and belief in myself, even if we didn't spend much time together. We exchanged many phone calls and emails. Unfortunately and fortunately, I had just missed that year's fellowship application deadline. To be honest, I was bummed because I didn't want to wait a whole year as I might lose my nerve, or I might burn out before I even begin. But this application was no small task. It was a work of heart, of memories, of hurts that healed and shaped me, and of new adventures ahead.

Think bigger. Think differently. These Bush Fellowship principles were new concepts for me in my little isolated world. I am imaginative and creative, so the thinking or dreaming part wasn't hard, but creating the action steps to a new possible reality— that was terrifying.

I was still applying my Blandin skills, new concepts and understanding of self in my everyday life. Knowing I am a trained ambivert with more of an introvert personality, this new idea of meeting SO many new people and building relationships seemed exhausting to me. I mean I crave authentic and deep relationships so that part excited me but the figuring out who are friends and who are acquaintances sucked my energy level to 0.

My mentors rightly advised me to go through the Bush Fellowship application process. That even if I didn't get it, the process alone would be a great eye opening and self learning experience. The application questions address you, as a human and community leader, as well as your dreams for yourself. They are very thought provoking. Healthwise, I am quite in tune with my body and medical conditions. When you start a journey at age seven and every other day therapists assess your pain levels, your conditions, and how you feel, rating all different layers of self becomes ingrained. Some questions seemed easy to answer, but when I edited and carefully reread my words, I questioned whether they truly reflected what I believed about myself and the world around me.

Each round of application questions went deeper and deeper, poking into areas of life people seldom let themselves dream about. It was hard work to allow the "what ifs" take over and release the practical, preprogrammed mentality. At one point in the process, I had a voluntary coaching session with an assigned one-time mentor. I psyched myself up for this great adventure with another pro. My other two Fellow mentors were amazing, so this person must also be, right? We only had 45 minutes on the phone. As a talker, this limited amount of time wasn't enough to build a relationship and shared meaning. I planned to share my story highlights with impactful words that convey my life experience in a few minutes. With the rest of the time, we could converse about my proposed Fellowship plan. Everything started great, until it wasn't. Sharing my story and all the hard work involved with becoming a music educator, as well as my community leadership training, went great. We had commonalities as fellow educators, and even laughed a few times. I thought we were grooving on the same page until I brought up the travel portion of my fellowship. I had let myself dream, and in my plan I wanted to go to Champaign-Urbana, IL; Amelia Island, FL; Berkeley, CA; and Sweden. I explained how this was a HUGE pipe dream as I had never flown before. If you have seen any news in the past few years, you will know that the air travel industry is not friendly to wheelchair users. It is improving, but the huge chance a wheelie takes in having their chair damaged is astronomical. Then there are the aisle chairs and lack of bathroom facilities. The horror stories shared by wheelie friends and strangers are enough to keep you up at night and away from airplanes. I am SO passionate about this work and my desire to wheel on roads and paths where other disability advocates have wheeled, to make today's life as good as it is. They endured sit-ins and constant battles with politicians to create: Section 504, the civil rights statute that prevents discrimination against students with disabilities in all federally funded schools; Individuals with Disabilities Education Act (IDEA), the federal law that governs special education; and the Americans with Disabilities Act (ADA), a civil rights law prohibiting discrimination based on disability. I want to wheel in these same places and pay my respects and thanks. I want to be inspired to take my work to levels that make our world even better for students and families wheeling alongside me today, and behind me in generations to come. I couldn't wait to experience the insightful conversations this mentor and I would have about passionate dreams coming to a reality.

Introducing ableism- the prejudice or discrimination against people with disabilities due to the belief that they are inherently inferior or need to be fixed by non-disabled people.

Instead, she said I was full of fear as she has an acquaintance who uses a chair and flies for business all the time. Therefore, I am letting my fear stand in my way because someone she knows flies all the time. First of all, yes, I can admit there is some fear involved. Anyone doing something new for the first time fears the unknown. I'm not unique in my fear. Second, just because one wheelie can do a certain activity, or does it often, does not mean another can do the same activity. In this conversation I was completely stopped in my tracks and retreated into my innermost parts. I was sharing with another human some of my deepest dreams and ideas, and bam— smacked right in the face with hard core ableism. I just agreed to her continued drivelings about my life and all my fears, hoping she would drop her bone and give me better help and insight into my writing and application process. I was wrong. I just shut-down to protect myself from the onslaught of hurtful words from a stranger; someonel would never meet or engage with again.. The sting was real and deep because I had not prepared myself for this possibility. To be honest, during this phase of the application process, I was in a more sheltered and isolated hospital and rehab space with only close friends, family, and physical rehab minded people. The world outside the rehab sphere can be very harsh and full of negative assumptions. After years in an ableist world, I consciously and routinely prepare myself for the what ifs around people's biases and judgements about my life, choices, or fears.

Looking back, I know this conversation likely offered abundant teachable moments and self advocacy, but because I did not fully prepare myself, it was a hard experience that I feared sharing. It took me several days to open up to my main Fellowship mentor. Our phone call was amazing, as she listened to me and called out the phone "mentor" on how she lost sight of her job and responsibilities to me as an applicant. I am very thankful for her approach to helping me heal, and her ability to see my hurt and help me use it to ignite my work even more. Even though these were hard conversations to heal from, I am thankful for the experience as it gave me even more purpose and passion to pursue further knowledge and leadership in disability advocacy and activism.

My surgical medical leave ended just before the holiday break in December 2019. After being out since the beginning of the school year with my knee replacement revision at Mayo, I returned to music teaching part time. I made my classroom a safe place by wearing shin guards and a Stop Sign knee wrap that my OT and DJ created for me. My caseload included some of our most physically close students with a wide range of disabilities and needs. We needed to make sure that the kids who didn't understand or practice respecting physical bubbles, understood that Ms. U was back but more fragile than when she last saw them. It was great being back in my classroom and second home, and back with my students who truly reminded me why I push forward and through so many obstacles to do what I have been called and love to do.

After being back for several weeks, my principal called. The COVID 19 virus had made its way to the US, and he told me NOT to come in to work the next work day as he was concerned that all my immunocompromising conditions would put me at great risk. In fact, he wanted me out of his building as soon as possible that day. I was very thankful for his abundance of care and caution for me as a human being and for my safety as his employee, so I could stay home and transition my apartment into my new remote music studio. This was heartbreaking, as I just completed one of my most fun lessons for my K—5 students based on St. Patrick's Day celebrations with games, dances, and activities that really could not be replicated with a substitute teacher. Little did I realize how much more heartbreak and change was ahead.

The early days of teaching remotely during the COVID-19 pandemic are a blur of exhaustion, worry, and also excitement for new challenges to more robustly apply my Masters of Ed in Technology Integration knowledge. My everyday life, which is semi-isolated due to lack of accessibility and my superhero-like, overwhelming schedule now became even more isolated due to my immune system conditions. My life and daily tasks became completely upended. I was thankful that I could still see my friend DJ and my PCA, as they were both single ladies abiding by the new protocols of masking and distancing. This was SO important for me as my teaching was stressful and less engaging, since music teachers were to focus on content and engage when we can with no real expectations. Reading and math were prioritized as the world pivoted to at-home learning using technology. Not seeing my students' faces, singing with them, or hearing their laughter was deafening.

Many months into the pandemic and lockdown I remember a great conversation with Jaime, my fellow wheelie friend, about the topic of isolation and how disability culture could help the dominant culture weather this storm well. We spent hours on this topic wondering how to help based on our considerable experience with seclusion and separation from community. For me, the exhaustion of living in added isolation and the grueling grief cycle our world was going through individually and collectively, stifled and nearly killed my creativity. As much as I knew our culture could help the non-disabled culture, I was, and still am, at a loss for words and ideas to help others live the life many of us have been called to.

The COVID 19 pandemic brought about a new level of isolation and concern for those of us in disability culture with medical needs. Pre-pandemic we had physical isolation based on inaccessibility in segments of society— restaurants, businesses, hotels and sometimes even medical facilities. We faced societal and human interaction isolation based on communication barriers, schedules, lack of accessible locations to meet, or lack of access to transportation. Adding another layer of limitation to human interaction and community involvement due to the public health crisis was a whole new level to our "Choose Your Own Adventure" story.

The gaps that were once small grew large. The availability and accessibility of technology, as well as the knowledge needed to use it, grew from a gap to a chasm. Many were blessed to have shorter transitions from work and life routines thanks to telework, telehealth, and the ability to connect with friends and family virtually. However, people who did not have these options available are still struggling to heal from the great isolation they experienced, beyond what many people can understand. Sadly, many are no longer with us. The depression and other illnesses caused by isolation, the political and social division, the lack of medical help, and COVID itself were just too much. All the stress and division has fragmented all forms of relationships and support systems. It doesn't matter where you stand, or sit, on these issues, there are hurts and heartaches that need healing and reconciliation.

My life connecting with others here on the North Shore is often based around food and togetherness. If someone is sick, you bring them food. If someone has a baby, you bring them food. If someone loses a loved one, you bring them food. If someone needs a break or a good laugh, you go out for food. Even as I write this today in March of 2022, much has opened up and the dominant (non disabled) culture is resuming "normal" life and expressing love/care, but many in disability culture or medically compromised groups are not at this level of community.

Chapter 18

Kiss the Beans

"When obstacles arise, you change your direction to reach your goal, you do not change your decision to get there." - Zig Ziglar

And then the fateful day happened when I got the Bush Fellow email!!! BUT, I could not tell anyone as we had to wait for official announcements to be unveiled weeks later. My Bush Fellow peers could tell their spouses, but since I am single, I devised a different plan for telling my sisters, four close prayer partners, and my dear mentor who had been with me since day one. I bought a can of Bush's Baked Beans, took a selfie of me kissing the can, and texted it to them. They unofficially knew my hard work and soul searching had paid off and the dream was becoming real! Tears of joy were plentiful with great adventure awaiting in my spirit.

Kissin' the Beans, May 2020.

Then the real work and more deadlines began. I worked with a public relations company, created a bio,and an artist made a creative rendition of all our headshots.

To be honest, the first few months of the fellowship, which should have been joyous and full of celebrations, became quite lonely, depressing, and isolating. My cohort and I had worked for months pushing ourselves to think bigger and differently, which included many trips and bucket list trips which were now impossible with the pandemic. I entered a stage of grieving that I didn't identify until months later. All our fellowship retreats and gatherings were revamped to virtual settings, a great alternative but not the same as meeting in person.

One thing led to another, then my fellowship took an abrupt halt. You see I am on minimal support that covers my PCA services, state health insurance, and rental assistance. Accessible housing is not easy to find in rural Minnesota, or really anywhere. All these systems have random rules and asset limits. The Bush Fellowship was considered income, even though it is not earned income. I now surpassed the income limit to continue receiving rental assistance and PCA services. I hired a disability lawyer using fellowship funds to fight against the archaic laws that don't include grants or fellowships as exceptions to income for asset limits. Many months and meetings later, after my lawyer wrote letters explaining my situation, the requirements for expending fellowship funds, and how outdated terms in the law were punitive towards people with disabilities,

I was able to move ahead with my Bush Fellowship.

I learned a lot about my services, the law, and the work of lawyers in the ecosystem of justice. But some days I felt very frustrated. As my other fellows celebrated and began their work, I used funds for lawyers and stressed about losing this amazing opportunity just because I am a wheelchair user who breaks the archaic laws for disabled people. Most days I make lemonade from lemons, but there are days when I want to stop squeezing lemon after lemon while pasting a smile on my face for the world to see. Even today, I wonder where my work and leadership skills could be if I didn't have to spend months defending my right and ability to accept this fellowship. We will never know. I'm confident that through my story more people are better aware of the limitations and discrimination still written in the laws, policies, and procedures that impact lives.

Chapter 19

See me...All of Me

"Be yourself; everyone else is already taken."
- Oscar Wilde

During my Bush Fellowship, I began to research and enter into disability culture again. Due to the pandemic, this was done virtually through webinars, social media, and books written by disability activists and advocates. Part of our leadership journey is to learn about ourselves including our unconscious biases.

I attended my first Abilities Expo virtually. I had heard of these amazing intersections of all things disability, but they were always held in other states, in big cities far away from my hometown. It was great seeing people both like me and different from me living life, sharing their stories, and promoting disability products not seen in mainstream media. Seeing people like myself was refreshing, but to be honest, it was also very awkward at first. I would say about 80% of the people on camera were visibly disabled; you could see their wheelchair, indicators they were blind, or the captioning and ASL interpreters for the d/Deaf or hard of hearing. I experienced this world during very short seasons in college or other professional settings, but never in my home on a screen for three days.

One of the main presenters was Alice Wong, the author and founder of the Disability Visibility Project. Alice was interviewed by a Black disabled DJ and advocate on this session. While Alice talked about struggles and stories throughout her interview, I felt very connected to her even though our medical journeys are very different. Then the interviewer asked her what it was like to be an Asian American in a powerchair, and what followed next for me is truly a pivot point. Both Alice and the DJ described the discrimination they dealt with not just as a wheelie, but more so because of their skin color. It is here that I finally saw and understood my white privilege. Until this point I was seeing white privilege mainly as an ableism issue, but oh how wrong I was in combining the two. After this interview, I read Alice Wong's book *Disability Visibility: First-Person Stories from the Twenty-First Century*, a collection of many disabled people's different perspectives of life. Many were emotionally hard to read, but I am glad I pushed through as their stories increased my empathy, understanding, and curiosity.

This pivot point helped me, as a Bush Fellow, better understand the work my Intercultural Development Inventory (IDI) Coach had been doing on my personality traits. IDI is an assessment tool which helps you identify how you handle different situations, as well as uncover biases in your thinking and actions. I am a minimizer, which means I try to minimize differences between me and others to find common traits or bonds. This makes complete sense in my upbringing as one of few wheelchair using kids in my rural town, and college life as well. I always felt the need to prove I was just like everyone else to be accepted, and downplay my differences in order to hopefully be seen as equal. When I saw people of color that were disabled and fellow wheelies,

I maybe glanced and saw they were a different race or ethnicity than myself, but my very medical brain went into guessing their diagnosis or finding similarities in our stories to bond over. I didn't think or ask about their struggles, or differences in their lived experiences around their race. After more exposure to events and opportunities, I learned SO much more about the hardships and discrimination disabled people of color face in the healthcare system, which includes obtaining quality health insurance.

During conversations with my fellow wheelie friend Jaime, I felt safe enough to share these hard, truth-filled realizations about myself, and how I saw and treated others. Having scales removed from your eyes can be freeing and exciting, but it can also be filled with remorse and sadness. I am so thankful to be in these awkward-to-me spaces where I can learn, grow, and ask questions. Times of self reflection and, more importantly, converting these feelings into new actions is hard and humiliating at times. We all have cycles of success and failure. But we learn by seeing something unjust, determining our part in eliminating those thoughts and/or behaviors, and then living it out.

Reflection:

A concept Jaime and I discussed in some loose terms at the time was medical model versus social model. The medical model is what I grew up in. My definition is that our disease or accident has broken our body and we need to be fixed to fit into general society. I see the social model as the inaccessible world around me, which disables me more than my disease or accident does. Recently, many new articles and discussions have popped up in my social media feeds about these two concepts. These terms and definitions really helped me understand more of what I felt from such a young age, and gave me vocabulary to start conversing with trusted friends about my past.

I have always been and felt different, not just because of my wheelchair and medical conditions, but because of how I was treated by non-disabled people. I remember back in my college days during my general education classes, we took a course on American Indian Education (the class title back in the early 2000's). I remember learning a lot from my professor, not always through what she said, but by how she reacted or didn't react to things. One of the few things I do remember her saying was that she and many of her people had to "live their lives with one foot in the native canoe and the other foot in the white man's canoe". The constant pulling of these two forces often left you swimming in the middle of the two canoes because the pull became too much. This created a profound visual for me, as I have one leg in my wheelchair (disability culture) and my other leg standing (nondisabled culture).

I have had many discussions with dear friends the past few years as I have grappled with new understandings of self and the world around me. I desperately want people to see me...all of me. Don't see Jenna without my wheelchair because you miss out on the heartache, triumph, and faithfulness of my God through my journey. But also, don't see just Jenna's wheelchair because then you just see the medical issues, the joint deformities, and the lack of ability and miss the life full of abundance, laughter, fun, and passion to make change for others. I guess what I have learned the most about people, myself included, is that we all want to be seen and to be known. We desire authentic relationships where we can be safe to share and ask questions about things we do not know or are struggling to change within ourselves. We do not like when people make assumptions about us, yet many times we make assumptions about others. Confidence and humility is a balance we need to cultivate. Learning the tools to ask questions in healthy ways is key to authentic relationships and learning.

Chapter 20
Friends + Firefly = Freedom

"Come to the woods, for here is rest." John Muir

Part of the Bush Fellowship is learning and applying self care. Since all of my travel plans were stopped by the pandemic, much of my finances were open to other opportunities. I did some research online to find options for an electric third wheel attachment for my manual PDG Elevation wheelchair. Living on the rugged North Shore of Lake Superior in Minnesota, I knew I needed power as well as a tire designed for outdoors. The Rio Mobility Firefly 2.5 checked all my boxes. I called California and talked with the supplier directly, as I needed adaptations made. I have an elbow that is fused almost straight (my hook), and using it to turn, brake, or accelerate would not work or be safe for me. They were great to work with, and I received my Firefly 2.5 within two weeks.

Thankfully, I have an amazing, mechanical brother-in-law who helped me assemble my chair mounts and get the Firefly assembled in a few hours. It opens exciting doors to unknown adventures, but it also made being with humans a safer option as I could be outside without people pushing me and breathing their potential COVID air down on me. I could be more independent in regular life and adventure life.

Of course, some of the design functions of the Firefly coupled with my Elevation chair design did not work out as originally thought. Also, my arthritic hands were not able to flip the latches or lift the Firefly 2.5 to the on position. Once again I had a new toy, but needed non-disabled friends to help. I experienced a mental setback when things didn't work as planned, but the journey ahead was simply amazing and made me speechless.

I first tried out the Firefly in my apartment building with the help of my family— SCARY! Learning a new device that goes from 0 to 12

MPH in seconds in a small space is not advised. Also, going from turning on a dime to needing a five-foot turn radius was a huge learning curve!

Kim and I, Ely's Peak in Duluth, 2022.

One day I met my dear co-worker friend, who is also my former adaptive physical education teacher, at a regional paved trail, the Willard Munger State Trail. It was a fun and challenging adventure finding accessible parking with the space needed to work on my new toy, and learning to attach the Firefly 2.5. Traveling the trail was a huge blessing. I had been a tomboy and daddy's little girl before I became sick. Playing, hunting, fishing, agate picking, and spending countless hours by local lakes were pastimes I missed greatly. My favorite outdoor activities were replaced by endless hours in medical waiting rooms, tear-filled PT and OT appointments, and pain-filled years alone in my bedroom. This renewed outdoor freedom was a welcomed adventure; I hadn't realized how much I missed it.

Fishing with Dad, 1991.

On this maiden voyage of the Firefly to the Munger State Trail, we nearly had some spills. My wheelchair van attachment pin has about an inch of clearance under my chair. That inch isn't much considering outdoor trails have bumps and divots from seasonal freezing and thawing, as well as tree roots pushing up through the trail. I learned

SO much that day— trail etiquette, "naturally" things, more about my friend and myself, and about living life to the fullest. I went home that day with an overflowing heart and slept for hours. The fresh air, the new neural pathways developed for driving in new ways, as well as the new feel to my chair. I realized how taxing my adventures were on my brain: from wheeling my chair, to driving my van, to riding my "bike" and then all of it again in reverse. My brain was overstimulated and elated by new adventures and skills learned. Oh, and going 12 MPH without a helmet on a trail I just met...I do have a little daredevil streak in me.

It was fun to post my new adventures on social media. These posts attracted other friends and acquaintances who love riding or walking local trails, and led to almost weekly trips with close friends on city trails around my hometown. Other friends headed to the shore, and we tried the Firefly on dirt paths to explore an overlook to a local beach...priceless pictures and memories! The Firefly also traversed many bridges that I previously looked at longfully while driving by on the local highway. I was enjoying true adventures experiencing what I had only thought and dreamed about.

Grand Marais, Gitchi Gami Trail- Cut Face, 2021

Shared posts between me and my friends led to more accessibility work for me. I traveled up the Shore with my teacher friend, who later taught my Bush Fellowship mentor how to attach my Firefly. We had a great day on a new stretch of The Gitchi Gami Trail, and I answered the access and safety questions of trail developers. That day was full of adventure and new sights including a waterfall, a bridge, an accessible pit toilet, and amazing views of Lake Superior. New stories and lasting memories were created with two dear friends and supporters of my advocacy work.

Each trip generated more social media posts, which led to more trips and opportunities to share what was or wasn't accessible along the trail. It also resulted in my volunteer work of assessing more than 17 miles of sidewalks and trails within my small town. This was quite the summer project. Friends who helped me assess the sidewalks, curb cuts, and alleys will now and forever see these things through Jenna-friendly eyes. There were many hours and miles spent checking and rechecking my work. It was an eye opening experience. What I thought would be more amazing Firefly adventures in my town, turned into more accessibility work with government and agencies for years to come. There were amazing sections of streets or trails, but nothing that really connected or offered a safe ride for me. While I loved the city trail time with my friends, I enjoyed the regional trails more because I could see more nature and less city. I could also go faster!

Chapter 21

A CRT Just for Me

"The greatest healing therapy is friendship and love." - Hubert H. Humphery

The winter season in Northeastern Minnesota can be brutal. I was blessed to be off work this school year as getting through ice and snow in the early morning can be scary, unsafe, and very cold. The weekly or biweekly trips outside my apartment are a welcomed joy. The sunshine feels good, even if it is blinding from bouncing off the snow. Driving my van is an added level of independence and freedom. But oh do I miss getting out on the trails. Though It is spring on the calendar, it is not yet spring on the trails or parking lots.

I spent the winter researching new parks and trails throughout Minnesota. I have been invited to explore different areas and accessibility enhancements various state and local agencies have made. My upcoming spring, summer, and fall will be glorious with outdoor adventures, provided I have lots of travel friends and safe lodging options. I can not wait! With the long winters we have here, I have started researching an outdoor device that can handle winter conditions, as well as adaptive winter clothing/outdoor gear, because I want to be outside when I can!

Meg and I on our first GGT adventure, 2021

Meg is an outdoorsy, fun spirited, and outgoing friend. As our paths crossed more and more at church, a sisterhood developed. I watched her become a great mom to two boys who are my newest "adopted nephews." We started a great sisterhood with two of my former students and Pep Club girls. I became the advisor when I returned to work at my alma mater. We also became dear friends and sisters after their graduation as I watched them grow in their faith, marry, and become precious moms! The bond with these girls continues to grow through social media and in-person visits when they come home. Our friendship of four was a great time of fellowship, prayers, and accountability. Now, it is just Meg and I in town, and we have become very intentional about time together each month. She has a servant's heart and her love language is acts of service. She is a blessing to me in so many ways. She has been unknowingly teaching me how to ask important and awkward questions that go beyond the day-to-day, superficial layers of humanity. She taught me kindness and gentleness. Her Type B personality reminds me of dear Lisa, and the Lord knows I need to rub shoulders and live life more with people different than me. Meg reminds me in many different ways to slow down, be grateful, and laugh. She also demonstrates how to admit my humanness and my great need for God and others.. The coolest part of our friendship, so far, was when she shared her life story and educational background during a Firefly adventure. We laughed and laughed. I had no idea she was a Certified Recreational Therapist (CRT)! No wonder she was so great at outdoor adventures with me!

Meg helped me battle the winter weather with a trip to Bentleyville, our local outdoor Christmas light show. The Firefly was a champ at handling the snow and ice patches. It was so good to enjoy some independence outside in the snow. We also video called DJ so she could enjoy the winter wonderland with us. I love bringing my different friends together as it increases the joy and richness of life. Creating shared space with friends also reinforces the strength of my tapestry for the storms of life.

My time with dear Meg has been a source of great healing from previous friendships with people around my age. Rather than feeling looked down upon or as someone others didn't want to "become," Meg saw me for me, and embraced all the different fun we could have together joining the ranks of the Jenna-friendly support system. In order to be healthy, relationships must be an open two-way street. It is great to feel seen, known and needed. And having a friend you can give all your dark chocolate to is an added bonus.

Reflection:

Much of my life, local culture and relationships are based around food. When I began my Firefly adventures with many old and new friends, it was SO freeing and healthy to have other activities we can do within safe distance, meeting my medical team's guidance for COVID protocols, AND being out in nature with amazing people in 3D aka real form!

Now, instead of sugary treats, fried meals, and coffee at the center of our time together, the Firefly has created memories and deeper relationships. Exploring trails with trusted friends in town and out in the greater region brought freedom. Being at the mercy of a battery and technology was a bit unnerving to begin with, so having seasoned smart riders as my trail tour guides was a huge relief and support to me!

When spending time outdoors wasn't possible, it was friends and family who respected and honored my needs and restrictions that changed my life. Their actions spoke volumes to my heart.

My teacher bestie and Meg were the glue that held me together during the pandemic. I know God is ultimately my glue, but these two friends who live nearby and can be physically present, helped me move forward through the increased isolation and frustration with the ways of the world. They relentlessly kept tabs on me, and were willing to mask in person and meet virtually. We even did a full Bible study together using Zoom in the early pandemic days. Their selfless love and care for me spoke volumes to my heart and hurts of the past.

It isn't about agreeing on every topic the pandemic raised, or the varied opinions on effective protocol or individual rights. They choose to follow what I and my medical team believe is best for me in the current world situation. They are also flexible when I need to deviate momentarily to just be me, and give a hug when needed. There is also no need to continually explain and communicate my medical needs, which is a HUGE relief in these friendships. We all need safe places to just be ourselves and live life. Sometimes it looks or requires something different than your other relationships.

Chapter 22

Who Am I?

"I don't know what lies around the bend, but I'm going to believe the best does." L.M. Montgomery

Being silly on GGT at Gooseberry Falls State Park, 2022.

During the 2020-21 school year I taught general music and choir full time from home to grades

K–12 in two locations. This season of life was extra hard as protocols, expectations, and students changed daily. The burnout rate for our teachers was at an all time high with no end in sight. At one school I was the distance learning music teacher, so I had all the students and families who chose distance learning for the year, as well as students coming in and out of quarantine. Once we got in the groove, this style of teaching became more rewarding than the previous spring. These music classes restored the expectations of attendance and participation, so we were back to creating music together in virtual ways.

My other school used a hybrid approach. I taught from home while students were either at home or school with me teaching them through their chromebooks. Designing a music lesson with students scattered throughout the region, in various settings and with different expectations, was a tremendous challenge. The school year, especially the spring, passed by in a blur of life and world changes, and without programs or concerts to celebrate and demonstrate our learning and growth. It seemed everyone was in survival mode, completely exhausted and clinging to whatever helped get us through. This was especially true for teachers. . There were very few moments in this setting that I felt successful, which made it one of my hardest seasons of teaching.

Summer breaks start differently for all teachers. Many of us are pushing so hard to fit everything in and create lasting memories for students, that we end up crashing for a week or more once the students are gone, paperwork is submitted, spaces are cleaned, and keys are turned in for the summer. After this, most teachers of high seniority then enjoy some time off to restore. In my 16 years of teaching in public education, this was never my story. Every spring, music programs faced the possibility of cuts that usually didn't happen, but the ongoing stress and fight took its toll. The summer of the pandemic was no different, but this time it was about me—my health, wellness, and safety. I worked hard researching different bubbles or PPE (personal protective equipment) I could wear to teach in person. Our buildings were built back in the 1940—60's so wheelchair accessibility was still a challenge in some ways. The situation was compounded by needs for a single accessible bathroom and an eating space that met my doctors' COVID recommendations for me. Finally, in the last days of August 2021 the school district decided they were not interested in accommodating my medical needs for the school year. Since COVID laws and policies had changed at the federal level, I was facing unemployment and many battles of conflicting messages from the school district, teachers union, long-term disability insurance, lawyers, my medical team, and Social Security.

I'm thankful my long-term medical disability includes something as visible as a wheelchair so others understand I have a disability. COVID 19 showed me a small dose of what others with invisible disabilities face every day. My arthritis related immune system issues, the medications I take, and my Type 2 diabetes are all unseen disabling conditions when dealing with COVID 19. Early in this journey I was not sure I could take the vaccinations due to my compromised immune system and medications, so I lived a more isolated life far longer than the average healthy person. Eventually I took the vaccine and had no ill effects. That was a blessing as my body often responds unpredictably to seemingly harmless, everyday things, so introducing a new vaccine was concerning. I had worked with multiple systems and insurance procedures throughout my life and career, so the failed systems still frustrated me. Due to previous experiences with archaic systems, I wasn't surprised by the prolonged processes and conflicting messages.

During this season of waiting for final decisions regarding long-term disability insurance, I had no income. I had at least three months with no income and very few bills decreasing, except for my gas bill since I was home more and traveling less. I applied for Social Security Disability (SSDI) which also took three to six months for application processing. I looked into Teacher Retirement Disability, too. The time I spent on the phone waiting to talk to lawyers, system administrators, and my medical team for forms and medical records was long and exhausting. Not working was now my full time job. I ended up applying for EBT (food stamps). Of all the systems I worked with, it was the quickest and easiest process. Even thoughI knew I needed to apply for this assistance, it still had its mental and emotional impact. The people I worked with at the county were great and supportive, but the process, while easier, felt depressing and oppressive. We are all one accident, injury, illness, or world pandemic away from needing help for a season or indefinitely, so why do we make others feel less than when they need help? Why do we look down on and judge others when they are already down on their luck and struggling? Though the struggle is real, humanity has much to learn about how we should treat others.

After months of uncertainty, sleepless nights, frustrations and tears, I decided to retire early under disability. This is definitely not the way I wanted to end my career of music teaching. I hurt over the lack of closure or opportunity to say goodbye to my students and coworkers. No final programs or concerts, no final goodbyes, just a motion at a school board meeting accepting my retirement. A few weeks later I received a great surprise from my elementary school: a candy-filled potted plant of gift cards, and a tear provoking card from my coworkers. It makes me cry just thinking of this. Eventually, other retirement acknowledgements came, which were mixed blessings for a variety of reasons, but the lack of closure with "my kids" is still hard. Maybe this door will open again, or my skills will be transitioned into other ways of educating and engaging with students. For now, I invest my time and abilities into my LEGO robotics team and their families. They are willing to work with my medical team's protocols to keep me more safe during our practices and I can be remote during our competitions.

In my early days of retirement, I really went through an identity crisis. When so much of your life is spent preparing for this career, this identity, and so many sacrifices are made personally, medically, and mentally to continue in this hard career, it is easy to lose all other versions of self. I fought so many external and internal battles to become a master level teacher, as well as push through man-made barriers of ignorance and oppression. Now that the career was over, for now at least, what was the point of it all? Those were my raw and hard thoughts and feelings to process. Even now, though I am farther along in the grieving process, I still have more work to do.

At one point of struggle in my identity crisis, I was busy cleaning out classroom books and materials from my teach-from-home spaces. While mentally processing these changes, I was thinking of my Bush Fellowship and disability advocacy work. For years when thinking of advocacy work, I always wanted to provide training and education as a part of my future consulting opportunities. That's when I coined the term "accessibility educator". This revelation helped lift a fog and level of grief, because it brought my worlds of education, teaching, technology, and passion for positive change together in one role. This helped me refine my Bush Fellowship goals to be a healthier, more focused and effective leader. I began more eCornell courses for certifications in Servant Leadership and Psychology of Leadership. I started more self work both individually and with my inner circle of friends. I also consciously applied some of my new knowledge to meetings and projects within my community leadership opportunities. Change takes time and can be hard, AND there are occasional times when it can also be refreshing. When applying these new skills you can experience freedom by unlocking old, negative, and sometimes harmful behaviors or thought processes.

This season of change also prompted the completion of my two year Bush Fellowship. Once a Bush Fellow, always a Bush Fellow, but wrapping up the financial portions and commitments related to this amazing, life changing season was bittersweet. The Fellowship is an individual, transformative change process. As I am a very relational person, the end brought about sadness or emptiness at times. I loved reading my cohort's monthly journal entries to see their transformations, but I also missed the human connection that our virtual retreats and learning times provided.

Until this process, I did not really understand my wiring and how relationally built I am. I also read and studied the book, *Find Your People*, by Jennie Allen. This book and its principles were surely true before the pandemic, but they are even more applicable and desperately needed as we continue through the pandemic and post-pandemic world. The activities this book provides taught me more about myself, about my and everyone's need for inner circle friends. I finally had words for my deeper longing to be authentic in community and living out everyday life with others. This helped me continue to heal from previous deep friendships that ended abruptly, full of pain and self doubt. Reading this book, doing the journaling and workbook, as well as listening to the accompanying podcasts was refreshing and inspired me to even greater and deeper change. Life and leadership are hard. Working with and for people is challenging, exhausting, depleting, and a huge responsibility. AND when you have your reasons refined and a fresh calling to the work you are created to do, it is a blessing and very rewarding.

During my fellowship, one of the things I was most grateful for was the compassion, authenticity, and humility my co- Fellows lead with. We built an innate safe place where we could ask questions and be curious. We strived to authentically become better humans more in touch with the thoughts, beliefs, and work of others who are different and similar to us. I was given a great gift of time with two Lakota leaders. These discussions and learning opportunities would not have happened apart from this fellowship. I was also introduced to the term "abolitionist" in a training with a former Bush Fellow. I shared meaningful discussions and activities with first generation immigrants, which only happened a few times in my life. There were so many amazing opportunities for growth and change in these two years.

The other very important part of being in this cohort is the validation we gave each other when we faced the imposter syndrome. The Google definition of imposter syndrome is "the persistent inability to believe that one's success is deserved or has been legitimately achieved as a result of one's own efforts or skills." Almost every leader or human faces this syndrome. Many times we are held back by the fear and negative or untrue thoughts that this produces. I am so thankful for these Fellows and inner circle friends who helped me through many different times and struggles with imposter syndrome. For me, having safe places to be honest, real, and vulnerable helped give words, validation, and encouragement to the energy and unction needed for the next steps of my journey and Fellowship process. And in all reality, the knowledge, tools, and healthy relationships will be needed to continue this work far beyond the two year Fellowship. This isn't an ending, but a new and continued beginning.

Fishing with my Firefly, 2021

One of my Blandin brothers reached out about accessibility around fishing for the Minnesota Department of Natural Resources (MN-DNR). These were great discussions and brainstorming ideas, which led to me virtually presenting to over 100 DNR leaders and employees sharing my story as an angler who is also a wheelchair user. My preparation time for this presentation was full of childhood stories with my dad, brother, neighbors, and even my grandpa. I also showcased my adulthood friends, family, and PCAs who helped me get back into angling,spend time in nature and creation at our inland lakes. I shared Firefly stories and adventures with my new trail friends. This one presentation led to even more connections, presentations, and opportunities to share my story. I eventually worked with state agencies, local government and other disability advocates in Minnesota. The fire was lit in my spirit toward this renewed work of advocacy and adventure.

All of these connections increased my passion for the work ahead, but they also created more work. I found myself needing to practice self care and quiet time to ensureI was doing quality work in line with my current goals and objectives. I also had to have reality checks to make sure it was not just my story and my intentions moving forward, but that of others who I hope to impact- those alongside me and coming behind me. This is hard for my personality type, because when working with many agencies and levels of government, things can move very quickly with immediate deadlines or slower than molasses with lots of needed follow-up.

I often had to pivot and realign goals due to federal pandemic funds going to underserved or unserved populations. These pots of money seemed to cry out for accessibility work, because in rural MN very little has been spent on addressing accessibility, or so it seems. I am SO thankful that newly elected or transformative leaders seem to be adopting this mindset and truly listening to their constituents. Forward moving officials and increased access to funding added more urgency to the work in front of me. Goal setting and aligning my work is always a dance between pacing myself and external factors like deadlines and agency needs.

Pacing my work is a new skill and concept for me in "retirement." Developing healthier habits and setting boundaries around time and personal expectations for myself is a new challenge. Using my Firefly 2.5 as a carrot for me to get work done has made a HUGE difference. It also helped me plan my work according to seasons. I can complete more outdoor work, such as content creation and relationship building, during the summer and fall months. During the indoor, isolated winter months I can use screen time to create presentations, work on writing, and participate in online conferences and engagements. Making these new neural pathways and changes to habits and schedules has been both exciting and exhausting.

Reflection:

> *In disability culture we have a term called Crip Time. Crip Time means a variety of things, but for me it means that life and time has to ebb and flow. As a professional, I was taught you must be early to be on time. Trying as hard as possible each day, my body, medical needs, or lack of access would derail my ability to be early or on time. Also, my disease cycles and medications create different levels of exhaustion and energy, so my working hours rarely follow a typical business day schedule, but more of a scattered Jackson Pollock looking schedule. For decades I worked and struggled fighting against my body and its needs. I would mentally and emotionally beat myself up for being late to family functions, school or meetings.*

Now I can plan my days, weeks, and months using pockets of time in flexible ways to better accommodate Crip Time. My closest friends are also helping me break self deprecating thought processes by frequently reminding me that value and worth are not connected to our timeliness. They know my heart, and being late or needing more time doesn't mean I love or care for them any less. Many times being a few minutes late means I can take care of my body and its needs so I can be fully engaged and present. What a joy it is to be free from shame and worry by embracing who I am, and communicating with others about our needs as a whole.

Chapter 23
Jenna-friendly Spaces

"It is no longer acceptable to not have women at the table. It is no longer acceptable to not have people of color at the table. But no one thinks to see if the table is accessible."

- Judith Heumann

In recent years I have observed that for those friends and family who have or create Jenna-friendly homes, it has made huge differences in our relationships. When I first moved back to my hometown and was teaching at the same school as my oldest sister, we had almost weekly dinners together and watched a favorite TV show. Eventually her and her husband did a bathroom remodel, and this created an even more inclusive space for family gatherings. In contrast, my parents removed their bathtub and installed an accessible, walk-in shower. Unfortunately, the plumber reset the toilet in the nook between the shower and outer wall, which made my parents' bathroom go from Jenna-friendly to a not usable bathroom for me. This has hampered the amount of time I spend with family or my parents in their home.

Over a decade ago I became good friends with a couple from my church. We celebrated Christmases and birthdays together. We have gone through health and heartache, as well as times of healing and surgeries for all three of us. They rebuilt the husband's family homestead into a great one level home that is fully Jenna-friendly once I get up the step into the home. By popping a wheelie, I am in and out of their front door pretty easily with little help. Being free to roam their home, to get around everywhere, and to use the restroom whenever I need to has created many memories for us, and a deeper bond than many other similar relationships. Plus they trust me to have a key to their home which, besides my parents, has never happened. They, their cat, and their home have a very special place in my heart.

Most recently my teacher bestie built a brand new home. They built a single level home with a loft above their garage as an office/playroom for the grandkids. Their former home was also beautiful, but had stairs to enter. I had the privilege of walking their outdoor stairs many times with her and other friends to meet my PT goal of walking the stairs into friends' homes. Those few times were sacred and far between, since it was a lot of work and energy for me to climb the stairs. Many times our friend group would meet in her heated garage, which eventually was named the Garage Mahal. We shared many laughs, tears, prayers, surprises, and times of worship in the original Garage Mahal. Her new home was finished , during the beginning of the pandemic. While this was the answer to much prayer, many months passed before I finally saw the new house due to the pandemic and my compromised immune system. We quickly christened her new heated garage as Garage Mahal too when we met, masks on, for time of gathering and games. Meg and I even used the garage as a recording studio for a special music song for church. This was a very special time as we sang a song I wrote back in college. I had never shared it with a crowd that size before. There is a special bond between friends when you can meet together in each other's spaces.

Recently my teacher bestie and I just spent an amazing day cooking, baking, chatting, laughing until ya spit, and playing a game in her kitchen and home. I love working together in the kitchen with loved ones, as there is a bond in creating something together and then enjoying the fruits of your labor. Plus, being surrounded by the smells of soup simmering on the stovetop and fresh baking bread in the oven is like a hug that holds you both close together.

Previous church friends gave me the nickname Salad Shooter. I have a notorious, unconscious ability to deliver the punchline of my jokes when others are drinking their beverages, which makes them want to spit out their drinks. I always remind my dear friends that they drink at their own risk when I am slap happy silly. On this day my teacher bestie almost showered me in her bubbly water. Sorry, not sorry.

Chapter 24

Local View from 4' 2"

"Nothing about us without us"
- Many disability activists

Another new opportunity arose in the winter of 2022 when our community launched a new local paper after losing our local Chronicle several years back. A local writer and caregiver of her disabled husband, reached out to ask if I would consider writing a column for this new publication. They were hoping I would write pieces from my perspective and share my story as a local wheelchair user. This was a huge, exciting opportunity. I agreed to a column every other week. I wanted this amazing outlet to share my story and ideas, but needed to consider the other demands on my life and time. I enlisted the help of close friends to help me wordsmith my column title, and we came up with *Local View from 4' 2"*. Yes, my eyes are at exactly 4' 2" when I am sitting in my manual wheelchair.

Being a columnist has really helped me hone my skills as a writer. Every two weeks I get to share about recent adventures, changes in policies, and accessibility information based on inquiries of others. I also educate the larger population about current trends or vocabulary use within the disability culture that I am learning, too. I have great friends who help me edit, as having space for only 400-600 words can be a challenge depending on the topic. I am very thankful for this outlet and opportunity to share, as well as the feedback and opportunities that come out of this column.

Chapter 25

Systems

"You may have to fight a battle
more than once to win it."
Margaret Thatcher

I see now that I am a systems-driven person. I have been part of many systems and, to be honest, not healthy systems for years! Being in a small, rural community with an aging infrastructure means that most accessibility adaptations are added on, back door type accommodations. In many instances a call ahead is required to make sure the lift or elevator is working, that an employee trained in equipment use is available, or to have staff unlock the accessible door. Almost every area of my life involves more systems, more work, and more frustration. When systems are broken for the non-disabled world, then they are completely broken in the disability world. For decades I have navigated the doctor world, the therapy world, the surgery world and the medication world. Since they are all healthcare, you would think it is one world and one system...WRONG.

As a student, and later as an educator, I navigated all the systems to graduate top of my high school class, receive many scholarships, and work with Vocational Rehabilitation for accommodations and financial help due to my physical and medical needs. Due to lack of access in high school, my family worked with federal and state agencies regarding health and safety (OSHA) to get our school district in compliance. In college, I learned and participated in the system to address discrimination from many professors using the grievance process through the Chancellor's Office. As a professional, I danced between systems with unions, lawyers, and advocates to get basic job accommodations met. I continue to fight antiquated laws and state policies that are not inclusive or in tune with what it means to be a 21st century professional with a disability.

I started my disability journey watching my mom, mostly, fight the insurance company systems to get the medical treatments I needed when I needed them. I also watched her navigate the supply chain system during many winters. When I was little, I did not know how to swallow pills so she would crush my medications and put them in strawberry pie glaze. This product only was available in our rural town in the summer. We would stock up, but we usually didn't have enough to get through the winter or spring. In the late 1980's and early 1990's there was no such thing as Amazon or food deliveries, and we definitely did not have the internet for research. So my mom found the company that produced the product I liked best, and wrote them a letter to have more glaze sent to us all the way from California.

I'm grateful for the systems I've learned about, and those that have supported me. And I'm burned out! I am at the point in my leadership and personal journey that if a system isn't working for me, then I throw it out! I dissect the parts that do work or bring joy and effectiveness, then examine the parts, protocols or timelines that are ineffective within that system. Another element of this process for me is learning which systems I can help change and which ones I have no control over and thus have to just live with. To live with the systems in place, I learned to retrain my brain and not waste time evaluating them, as I have no way of fixing them by myself. Rather, I have to fix how I work within these broken systems.

I am a work-in-progress in this new mindset, as energy use and how I choose to spend my time is more important now that I am middle-aged. On top of my usual medical needs, I have the typical human aging process starting to amp up more. I am glad I have some choices on how I spend my time and energy. I already felt like my body was 90 years old at age seven, and now as my medical team watches to assess how the aging process impacts my body... Well, all I can say, in the words of my Scandinavian ancestors, is UFFDA!

Chapter 26

Above & Beyond With U

"I wanna see feisty disabled people change the world." Judith Heumann

For a long time I used the phrase "above and beyond." During my Blandin Leadership training days, I found a new application to this phrase in relation to the American with Disabilities Act (ADA). So often when leaders, owners, or contractors use the words ADA Code, they think and act as if this is what they HAVE to do and ONLY what they can do. If you look further at this law in context to learn the spirit of the ADA, you will find that one can go "above and beyond" the code to make things even more accessible. The term universal design has become popular in recent years, and this term encompasses designing spaces that provide the greatest access possible for all people. Many times what has been originally designed for the disability community has become a mainstay in the general public. For example, do you or someone you know use an electric toothbrush? Yup, the history of this device goes back to modifying oral care for people with physical disabilities. When shopping or in other buildings, do you use the automatic sliding doors or the power doors with the big button? Yup, those are designed to provide access for all people with mobility disabilities or pushing/pulling restrictions. And lastly, do you use talk to text on your phone or computer? Or Alexa or Siri? Yes, they are applying assistive technology from disability applications to daily life for everyone. Innovation is created and driven by needs. The reapplication of the innovation can solve many other problems and meet additional needs. Going above and beyond code is what is needed and allowed in all aspects of life!

In my Bush Fellowship, I originally wanted to work on starting Above and Beyond Consulting, but as my work continued to evolve and change with the needs of my local and regional communities, I realized my approach to advocacy held many opportunities beyond just consulting. So, I am branching out and creating a non-profit called Above and Beyond With U. This name encompasses my core belief of "going above and beyond" the ADA building code. The word "with" refers to relationships and community building. The letter "U" is a play on my last initial. This brand can encompass my website, social media, accessibility education, training, consulting, and this very book you are reading. The needs of the community are very diverse and expansive, so I want my brand to be welcoming and fundamental at its core. To create my brand, I tapped into the knowledge gained from my eCornell Social Media Marketing and Women in Leadership certifications.

I am working with a local website development company whose staff has been of great help in navigating this new world for me. They have been great mentors, asking tough questions about intent, use, and content needs. I love supporting local business, but even more, local experts in their field who believe in your projects and passions to help make the local and broader community more successful and inclusive. The staff has also been sensitive to imposter syndrome and challenges around content decisions, as I put my life out on the web, for all to see and comment on.

I love working with leaders, business owners, individuals, agencies, and governmental departments to thoughtfully discuss change, make action plans, and celebrate successes while learning from "failures." Lifelong learning is a core value for me. The process can sometimes be tough or exhausting, but the lessons and rich relationships are worth the stress and toil.

I am honored to finally have the main stories of my life on paper. I look forward to the future stories this book will help write. Our lives are meant to be shared and experienced in community, even when it is uncomfortable, inaccessible, and vulnerable. I have been blessed with some of the very best friends, my family, adopted family, and church family. I have been blessed with a community of all abilities and beliefs. I have been blessed with spaces and homes where I can roll on in and have all my physical needs met so I can just be me with all my frailties, opinions, strengths, and gifts. Every event, moment, and person has been hand picked to be in my tapestry of life. Some are long thick strands of steadfast support, encouragement, and deep relationships. Some are thin but beautiful strands that are constantly there. And yet other strands are short and vibrant, serving their purpose for the chapter or season they were needed in my life. I am thankful and grateful for them all, but most of all I am worshipful of the One who brought them all into my life right when they were needed,to serve whatever lessons or purposes they were meant to bring, and make my tapestry of life deeper, warmer, safer, more colorful, and fun!

Acknowledgements

There are so many people to thank in the making of this memoir and for all the love and support I have received in life. Names and details have been omitted in stories as a sign of respect and care. My tapestry needed all the different threads of life to create what it is today. No one story or person is more important than the other as the absence of one would leave a hole in my tapestry.

First, thank you to my parents and family. I know our life hasn't been an easy one but it has also never been dull. Thank you for all your support, love, and care throughout my life. I hope, if you read this, you are given an even deeper understanding of these adventures I have been on and continue to pursue.

To my medical team and family at Duluth Clinic/St. Mary's/Polinsky Rehab/Essentia Health- THANK YOU! While I haven't been a compliant patient many times, we have grown and learned together. To the doctors, nurses, and therapists who have gone above and beyond in seeing me, not just my chart...your impact lives on in my work.

Lisa "Marie"- there are absolutely no adequate words to describe the impact you and your precious family have had on my life and walk with the Lord. You have my heart and your home is my happy place. (Yes, I am crying...) And thanks for my partner in crime...Jaime!

Jaime, Bud-dy, you have been a constant confidant and instigator of adventure and change! I cannot imagine life without you and your wisdom, bravery, courage, and unquenchable thirst for adventure and creating possibilities for everyone.

All my school age and college friends...thank you for being inclusive before that was even a hip word. After so many of our shenanigans we should not be here today. And you're welcome- I didn't share ALL the stories or all your names. Thank goodness we grew up before social media!

To my teachers who believed in me, especially Fitz, Cherne, Kim, Linda and many others- you inspired me to a career of service in music education while trying my best for all kids at all times. Even when I failed miserably, you were there to encourage me and help me dig deep to advocate for my kids and myself.

DJ- Your compassion and care are second to none. Our endless stories of letting me borrow your legs, face, and talents could be a book of its own. You are a Godsend in my life and in the creation of this memoir.

6- you have my back like no one else. Thanks for the consistent, safe, unconditional love and support through so many times of change, growth, and healing. Your encouragement and ability to always make me laugh while chatting for hours has been a healing balm.

To my Blandin Family, Bush Fellows, and life coaches- thanks for the safe spaces to grow and change. Leadership is not easy and we can not do it alone. Keep reaching out and reaching up! Think bigger! Think differently!

Firefly Trailblazers- thank you for being co-pilots on trail and off-road adventures! We have gone hundreds of miles and there are thousands more to go. Let's go see "naturely" things, find amazing food, and share inclusion as we wander.

Friends, co-workers, acquaintances, and sometimes even complete strangers- thank you for showing up as your authentic selves, for letting me borrow your legs, arms, or height, for making spaces Jenna-friendly, and for pushing me to be and do better.

Beta readers- your hard work and encouragement has made this book a reality. Sharing one's innermost stories and heartaches can be terrifying but all of your individual perspectives and connections to my life made this a better story. Thanks for having grace and being gentle with me.

Tracy, my dear editor and friend, thank you for all the help and random hours of answering endless questions and comments. Your expertise and care of me and this memoir are precious. Thank you for prodding me when I needed it and giving me space to grow through this project together.

You, the reader of this memoir- thanks for reading my journey of life so far. I hope you found a place to connect, to laugh, to feel, and to be challenged to live some part of life differently, more healthfully, and more "friendly."

And to the One Who brings Life to this whole book and life. Thank You that You don't make junk, thank You for never leaving me, and for having plans and purposes for me FAR greater than I can think, ask, or deserve. Thank You, Jesus.

About the Author

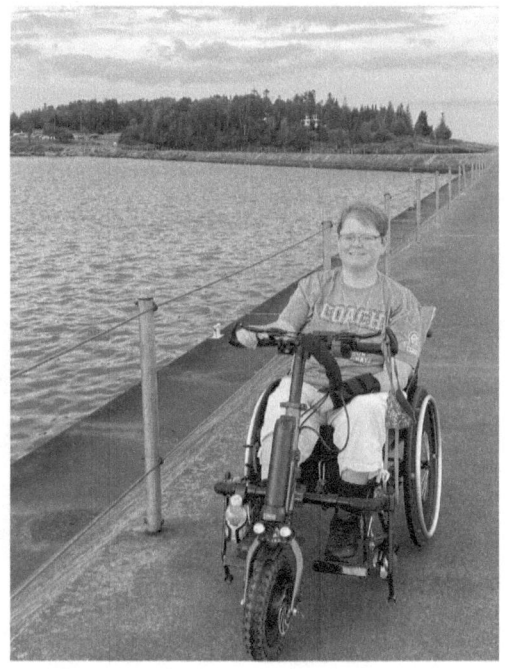

Jenna Udenberg

Jenna grew up on the beautiful North Shore of Lake Superior in Minnesota. She received her double degree of Bachelor of Music Education and Masters of Education. Jenna taught music to all levels and all instruments from elementary age to adults for over 20 years. Jenna has been a disability advocate since childhood. She now is working as a disability activist and accessibility educator. Jenna's newspaper column, *Local View from 4' 2"*, can be found in the Lake County Press and she loves working with others including her non-profit, Above & Beyond With U.

When Jenna isn't busy working you can find her out on the trail, fishing from shore, or playing board and card games with family and friends. When the stress gets high Jenna turns to baking and cooking for loved ones and co-workers.

Share your story with me!

I work best in community so I can't wait to hear how these stories landed with you. I look forward to hearing your stories and working together to make our spaces more accessible and inclusive for everyone. Let's dig deep and go Above & Beyond together!

<u>www.aboveandbeyondwithu.org</u>

@aboveandbeyondwithu